MATHPIANO®
Building Math Literacy in Music

Key Book

This book belongs to

My Piano Teacher is

Assessment Record

Student ID

			Center ID
LV2	Completed	Date ☐☐/☐☐/☐☐	

This book pairs with the MathPiano curriculum for students who have completed the Level 2 Assessment.
For more details, visit www.mathpiano.com

MATHPIANO® is a licensed program.

Join our community to receive full support.

www.mathpiano.com
Research Credits: BAAM Students

" **Everyone is entitled to read music.** "

MATHPIANO® - Key Book

Author: Elaine Chung
Copyright © 2024 by Erssa Group, LLC

ISBN 979-8-9916375-2-7

U.S. Copyright Registration Number: TXu 2-455-207

Published by Erssa Group, LLC
12356 Northup Way, Suite 111, Bellevue, WA 98005 U.S.A.

Table of Content

How to use this book:

This book is intended for students who have successfully completed the **MATHPIANO Assessment Level 2**. If you obtained this book without officially passing the level, please visit www.mathpiano.com to find a licensed teacher or agency near you, or consider joining the digital school.

Complete the key chart based on the diatonic scale of Western music. For reference, see the back of the book for detailed examples of major and natural minor scales. It is essential for the student to have a solid understanding of how each key functions in order to apply it effectively to the pieces.

1. Begin by filling in the 'letters' sequentially from number 1 to 7, without skipping any letters. Avoid playing on the piano or adding sharps and flats at this stage, as it could cause confusion or disrupt the sequence.

2. Next, review the key system and add the appropriate sharps or flats to the letters, following the example provided. Remember, each letter corresponds to a specific note on the piano and repeats through octaves, both higher and lower.

Ensure that your charts are accurately completed. Once done, the key chart can be used to complete your **MATHPIANO** worksheets.

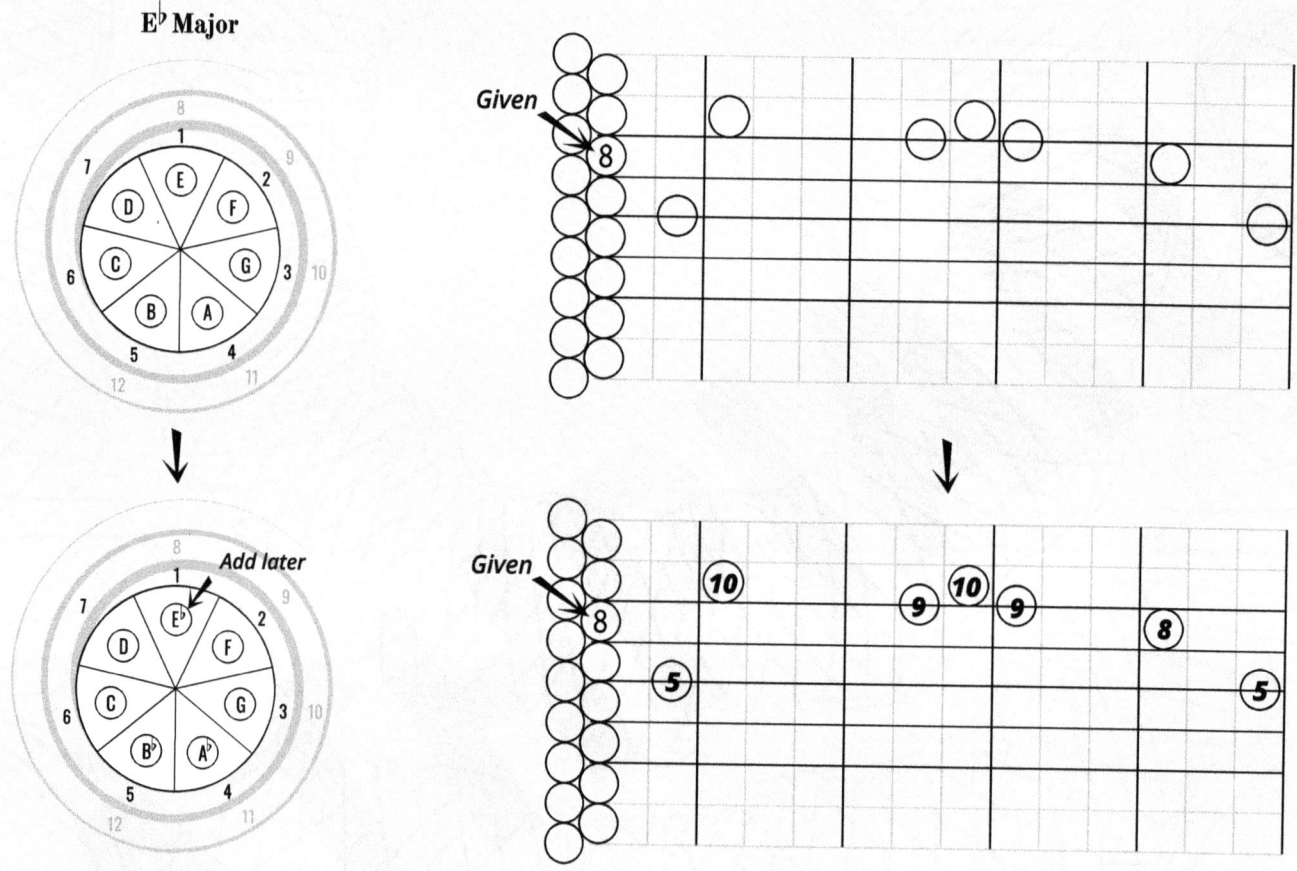

Arrows may appear on the song worksheets to indicate a half-step raise or lower based on the key chart. For example, if a number 1 (E flat) has an upward arrow, it should be played as E natural.

Raises a half-Step

Lowers a half-Step

Using this chart at the initial stage is the most effective way to prevent incorrect notes from being introduced before they become habitual, ensuring the correct tonality is established from the start. Good luck!

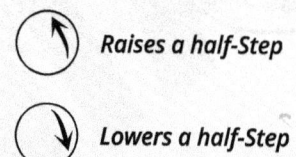

C + (a-)

#		♭
G + (e-)	1	F + (d-)
D + (b-)	2	B♭ + (g-)
A + (f♯-)	3	E♭ + (c-)
E + (c♯-)	4	A♭ + (f-)
B + (g♯-)	5	D♭ + (b♭-)
F♯ + (d♯-)	6	G♭ + (e♭-)
C♯ + (a♯-)	7	C♭ + (a♭-)

Key: C Major

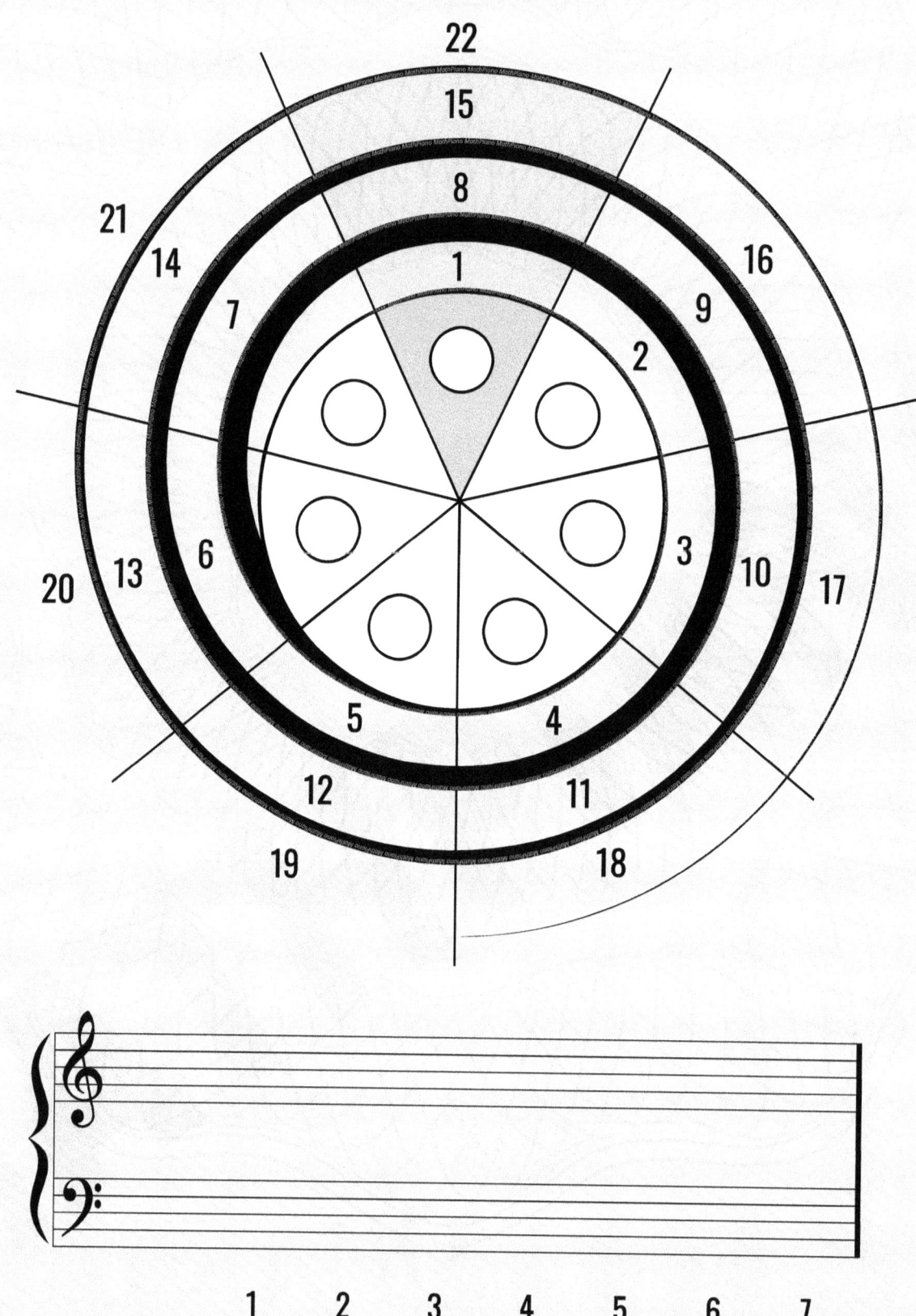

Key: A Minor

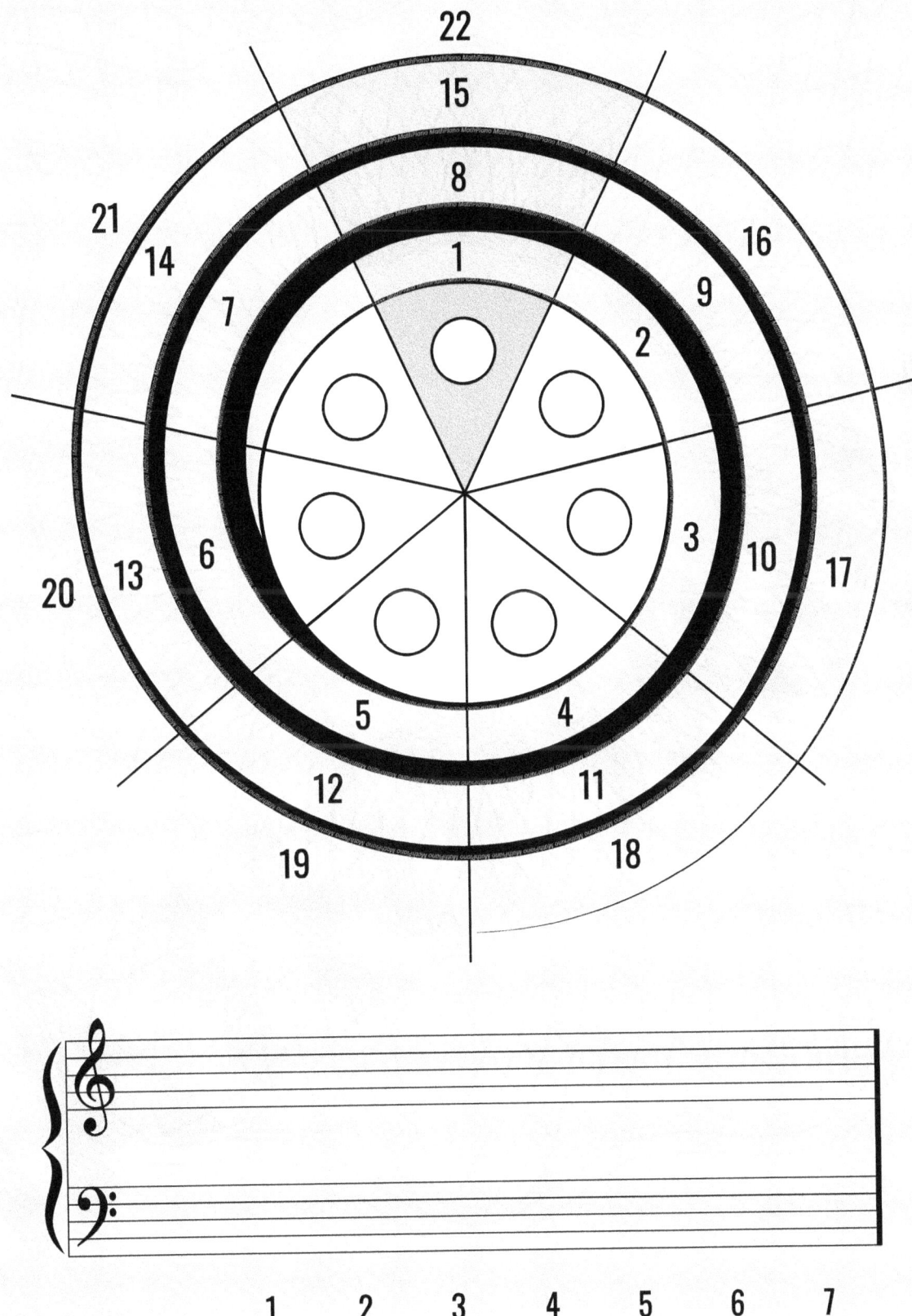

Key: G Major

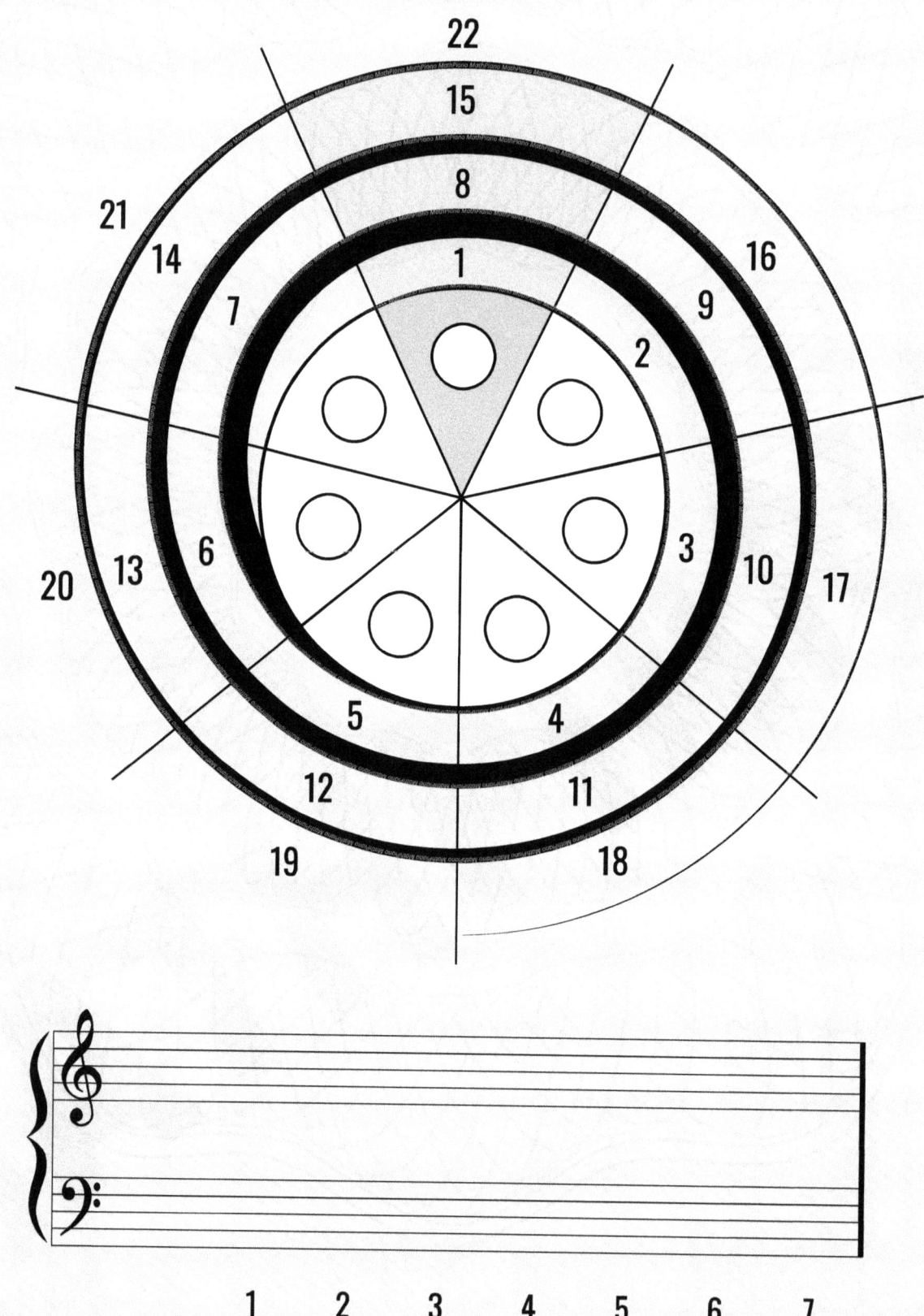

Key: E Minor

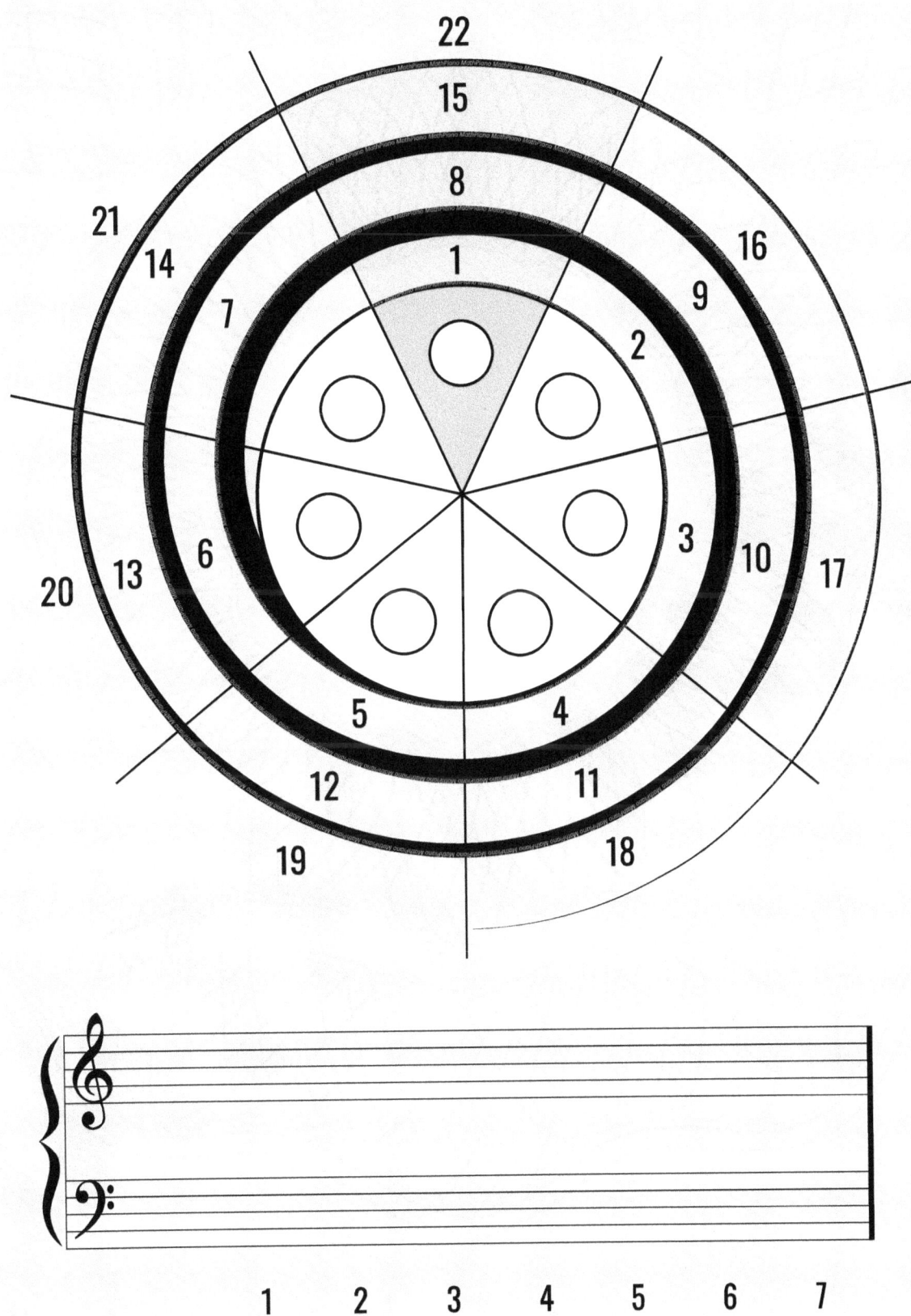

9

Key: D Major

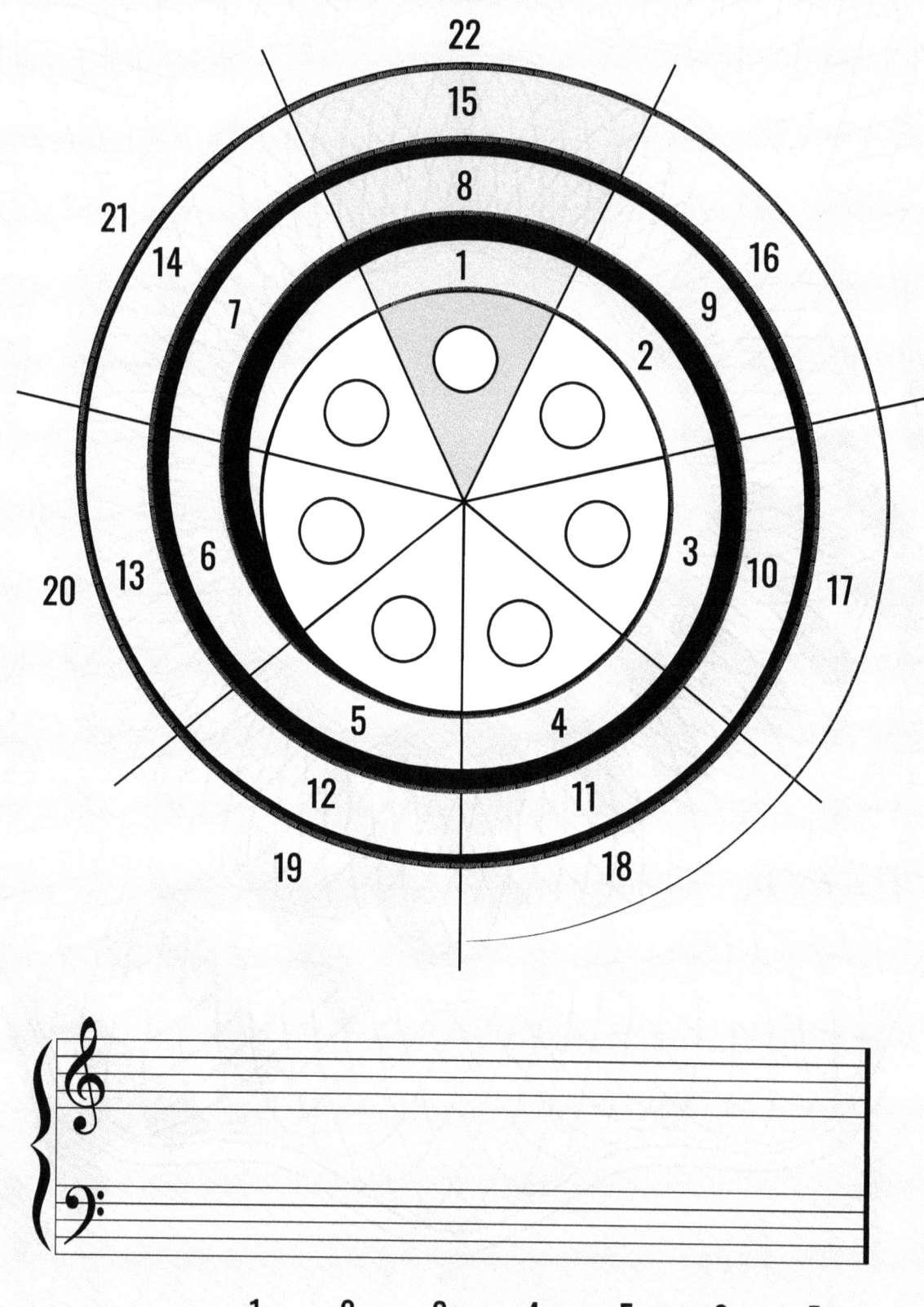

Key: B Minor

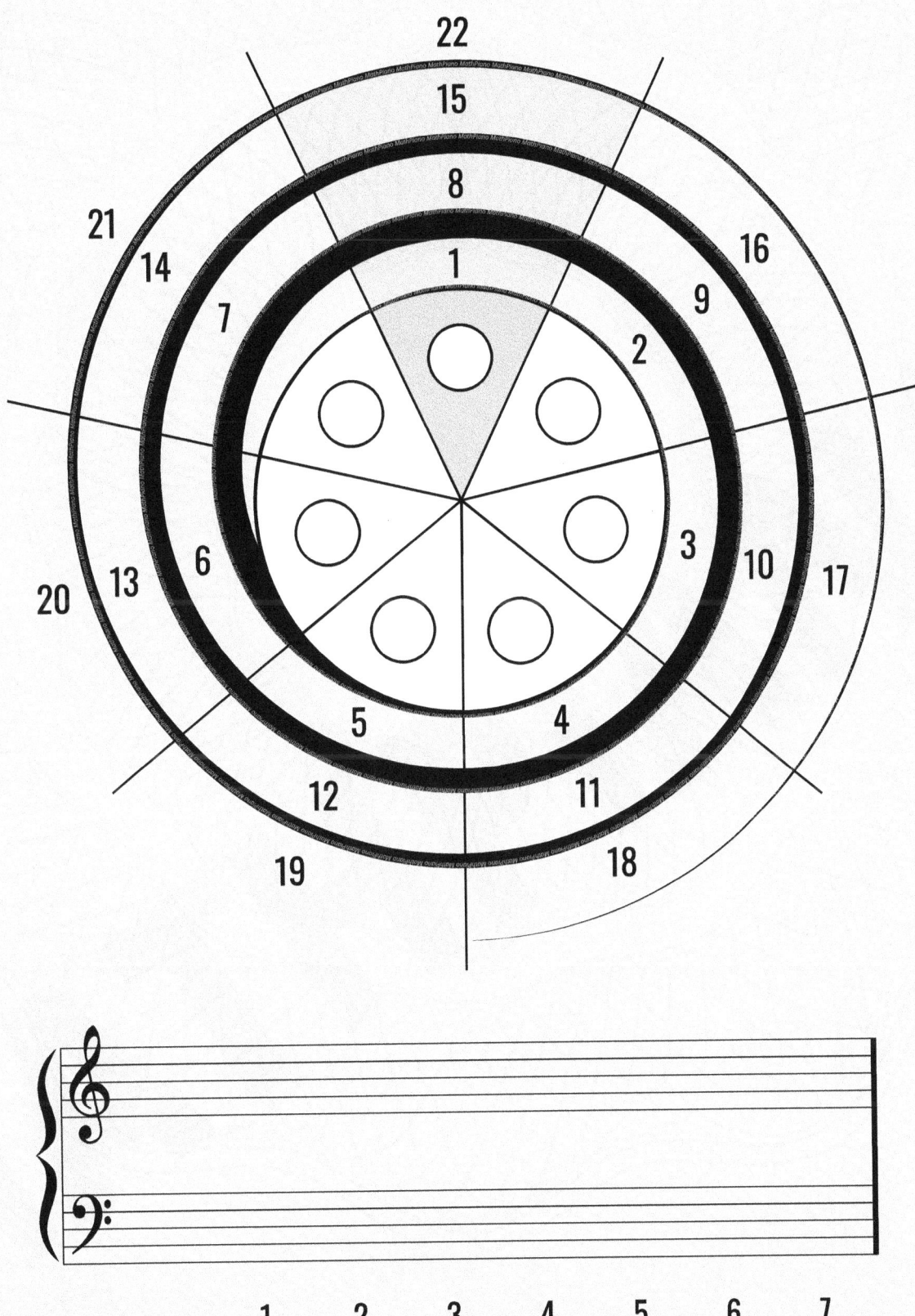

Key: A Major

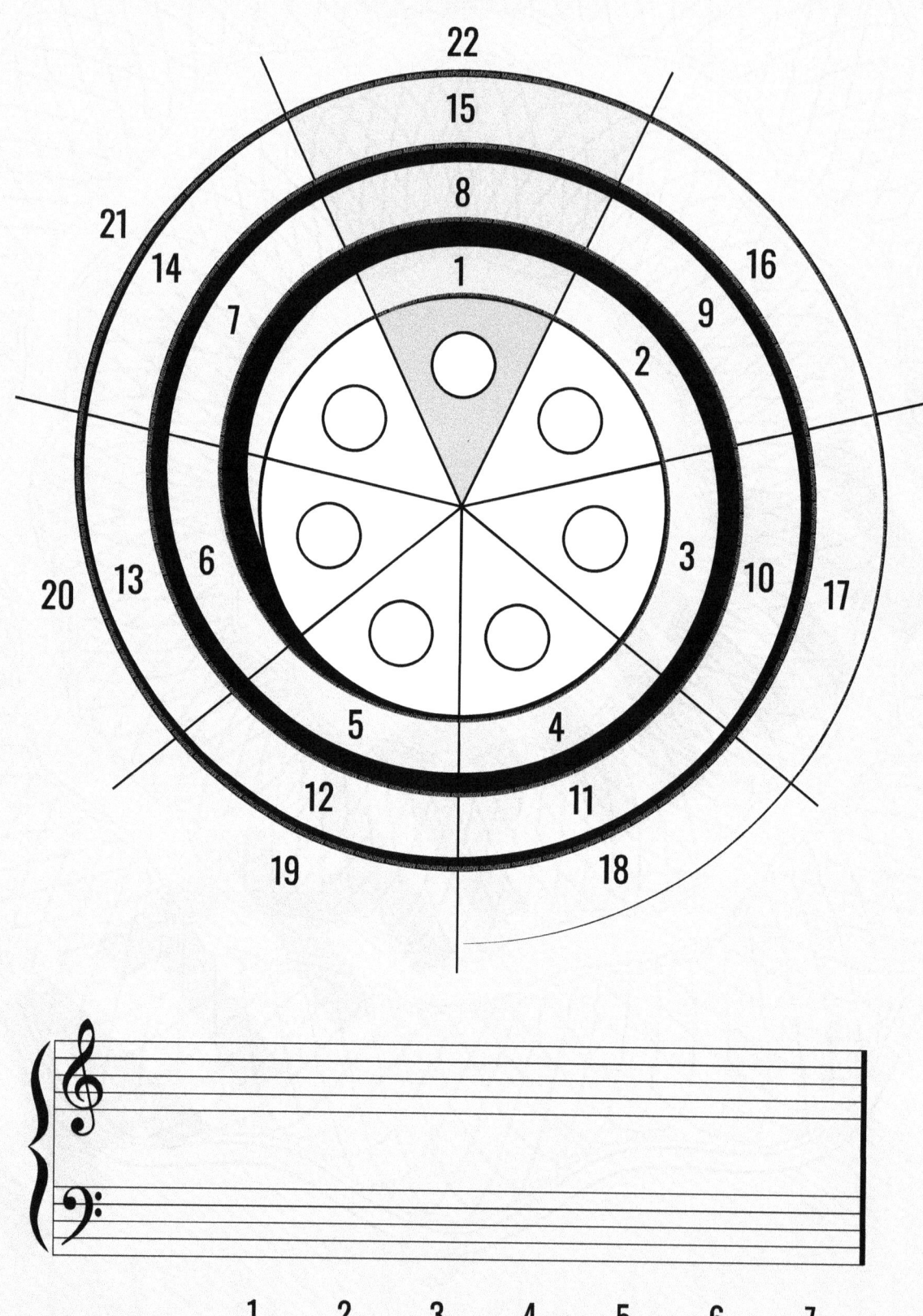

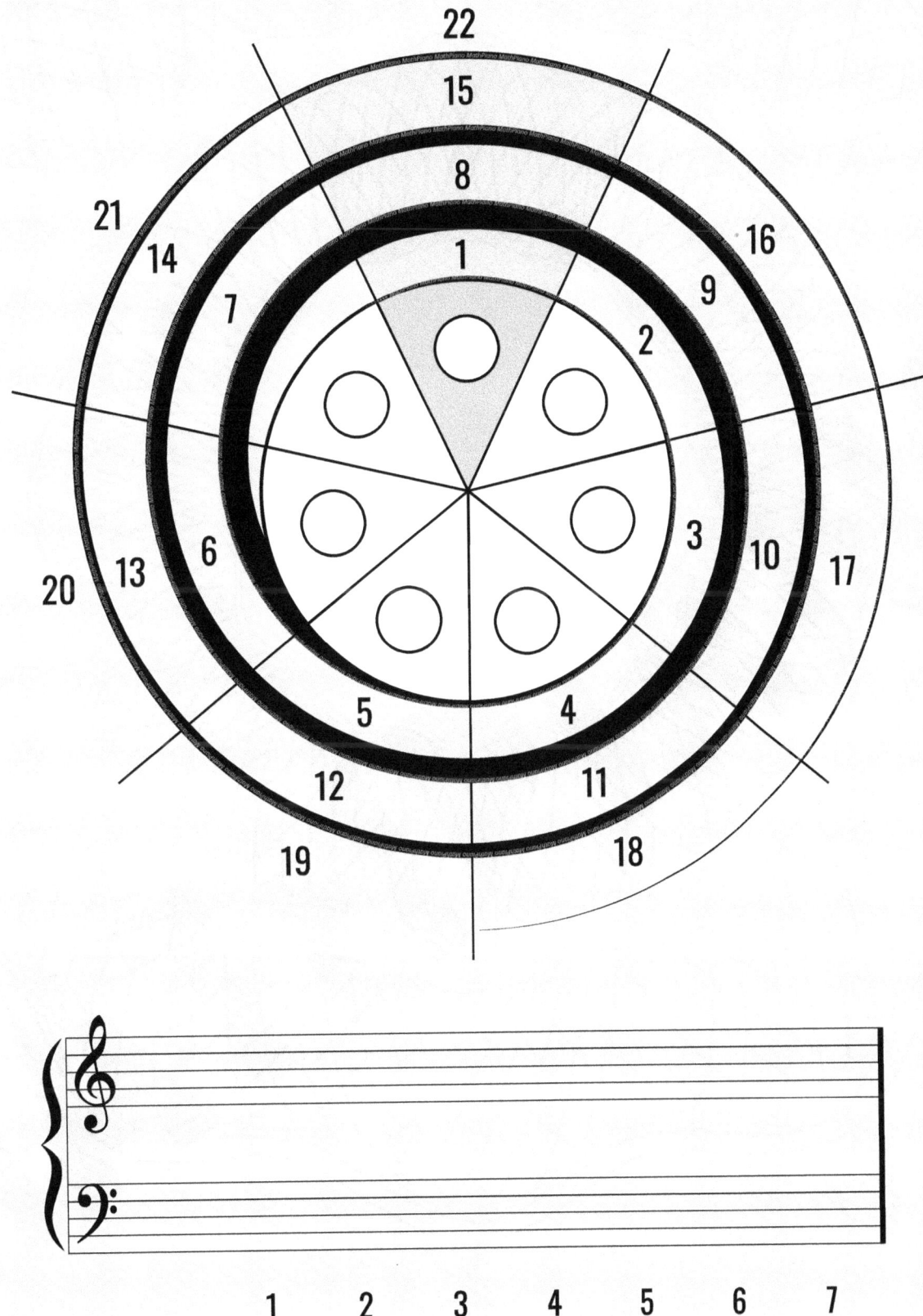

Key: F♯ Minor

1   2   3   4   5   6   7

Key: E Major

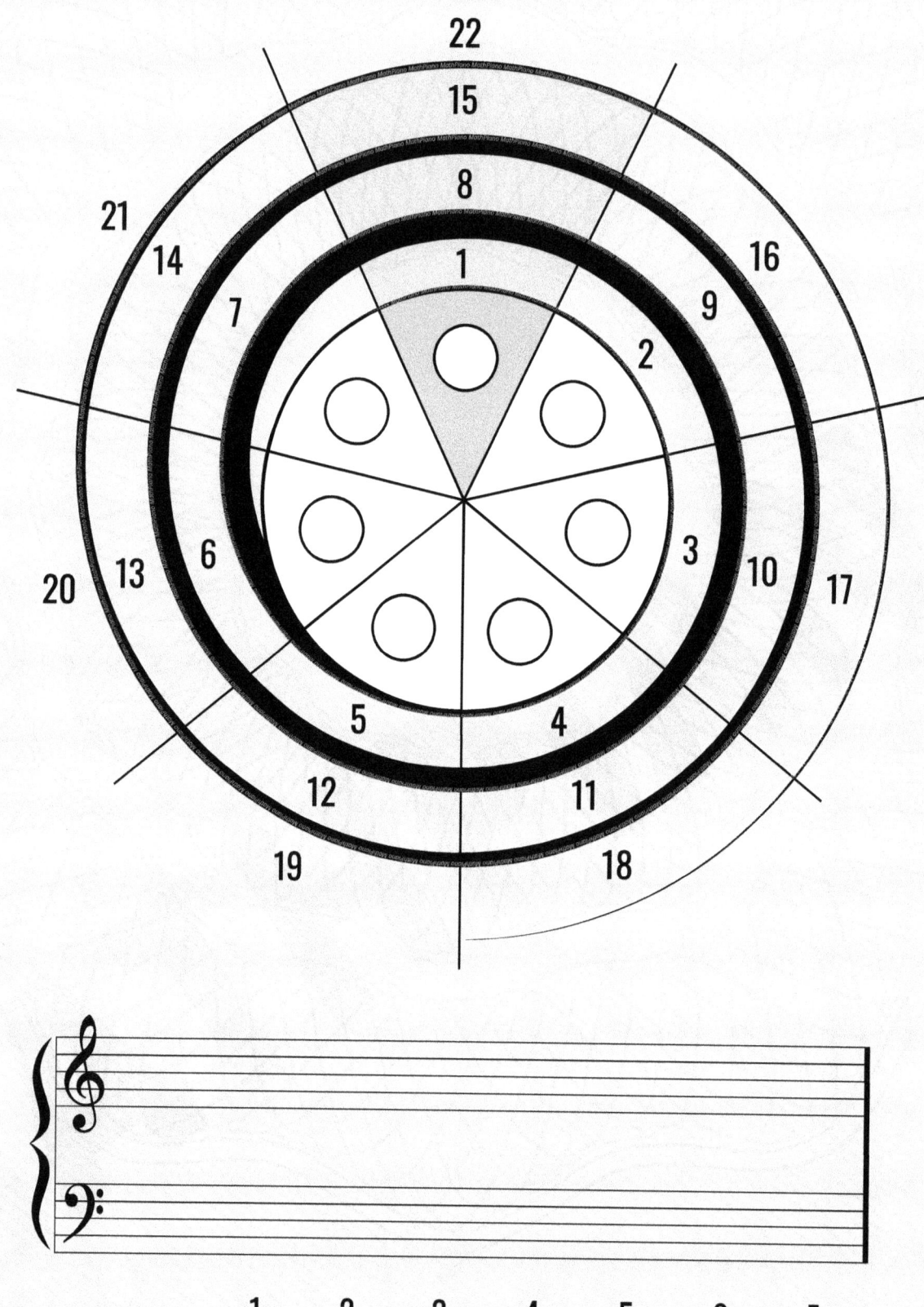

Key: C#Minor

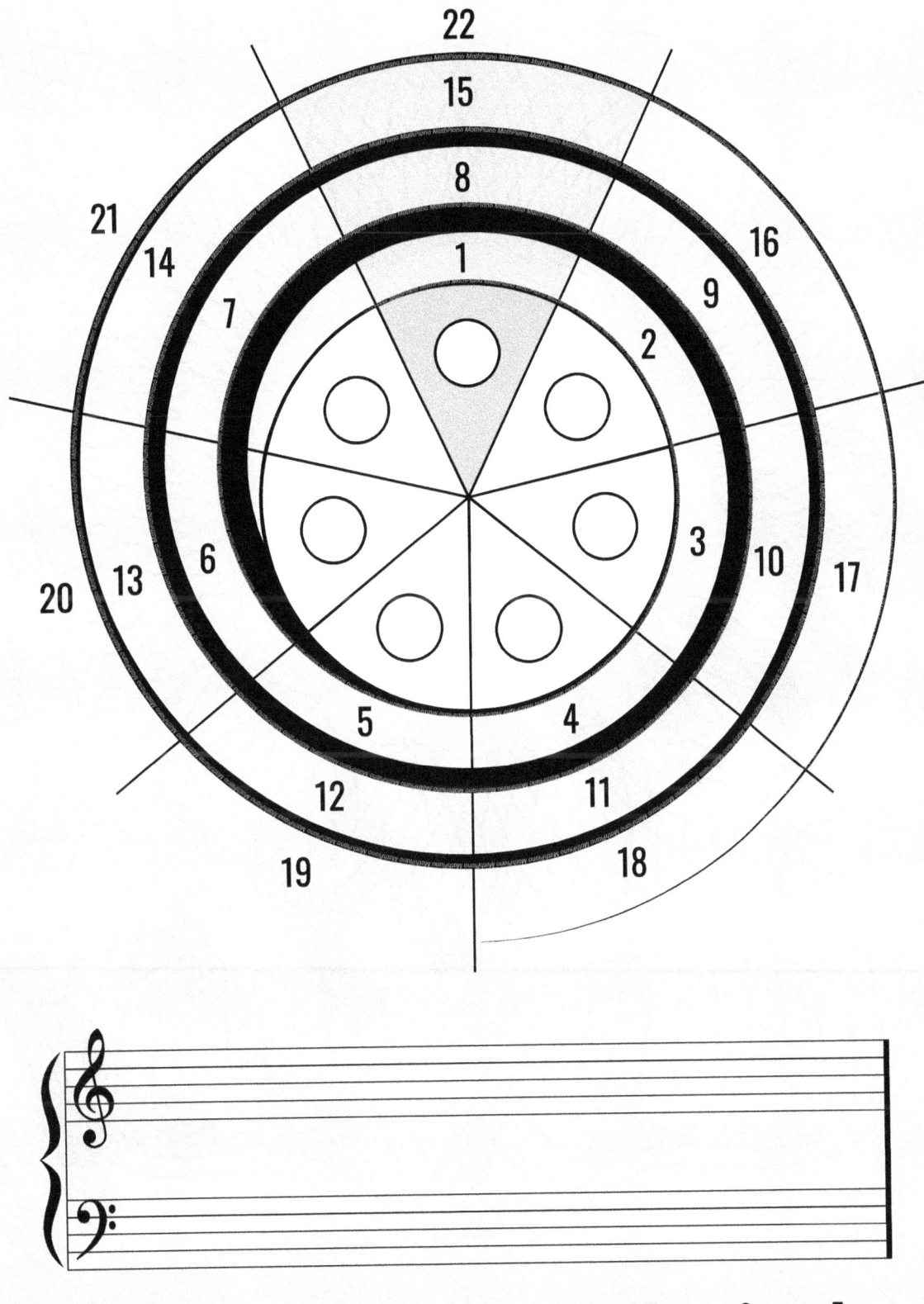

Key: B Major

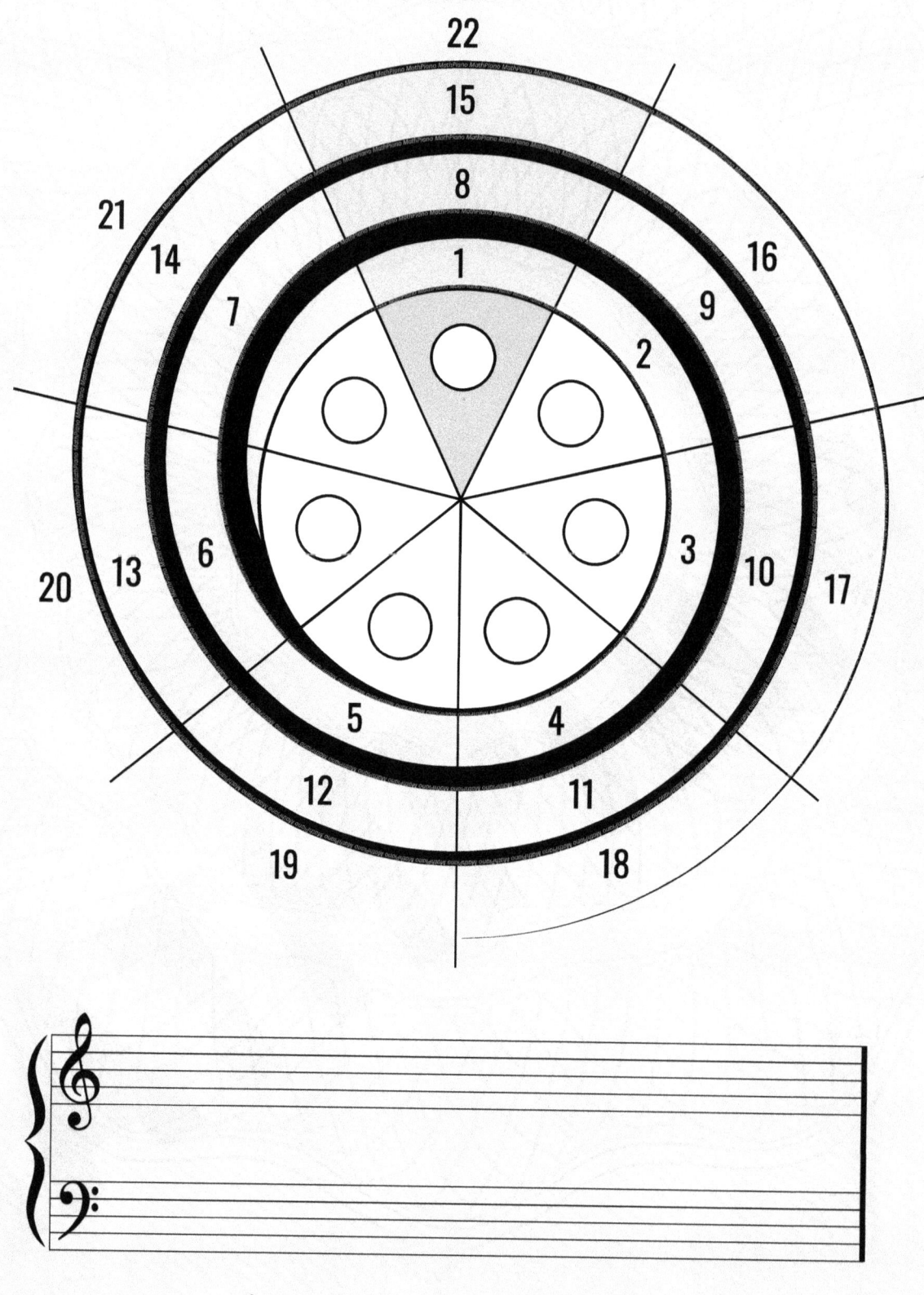

Key: G# Minor

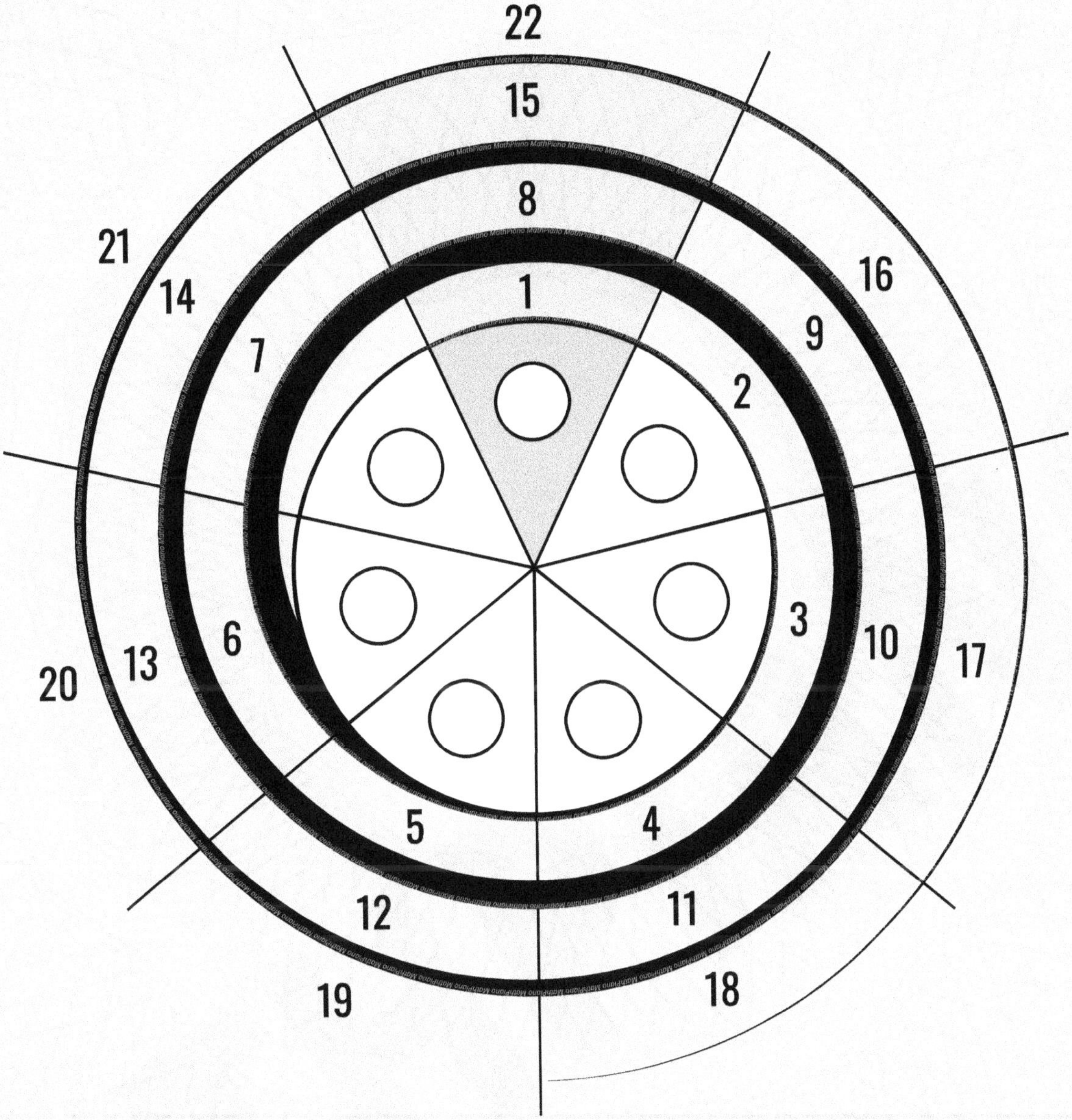

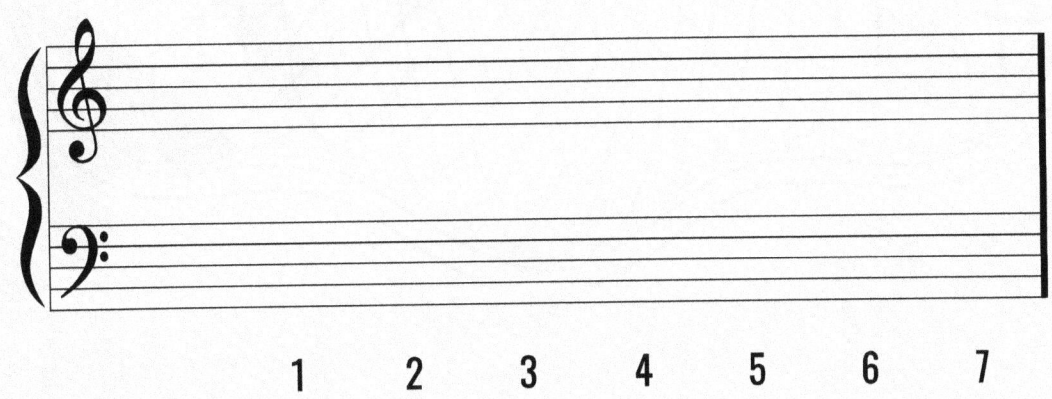

Key: F#Major

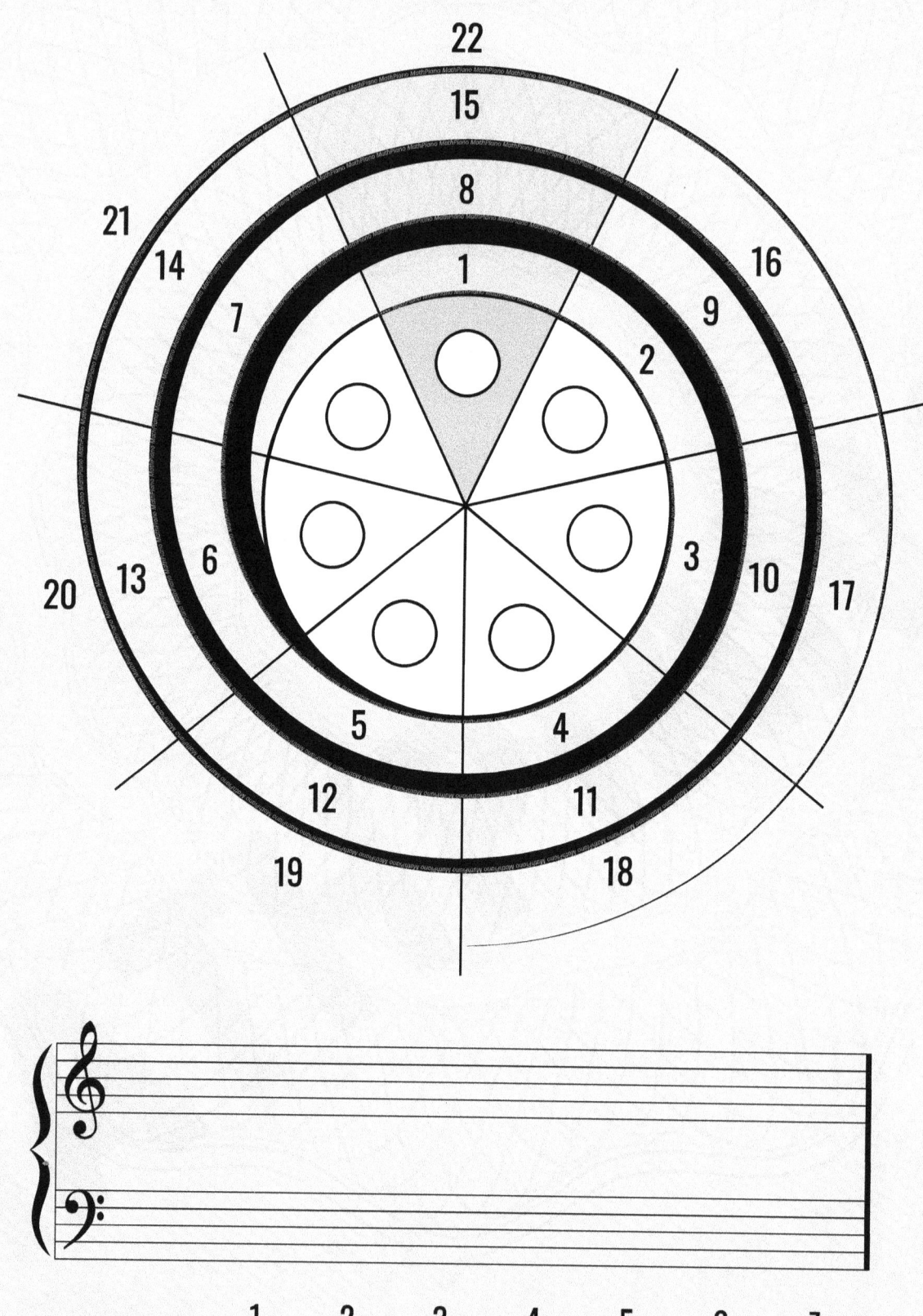

Key: D♯ Minor

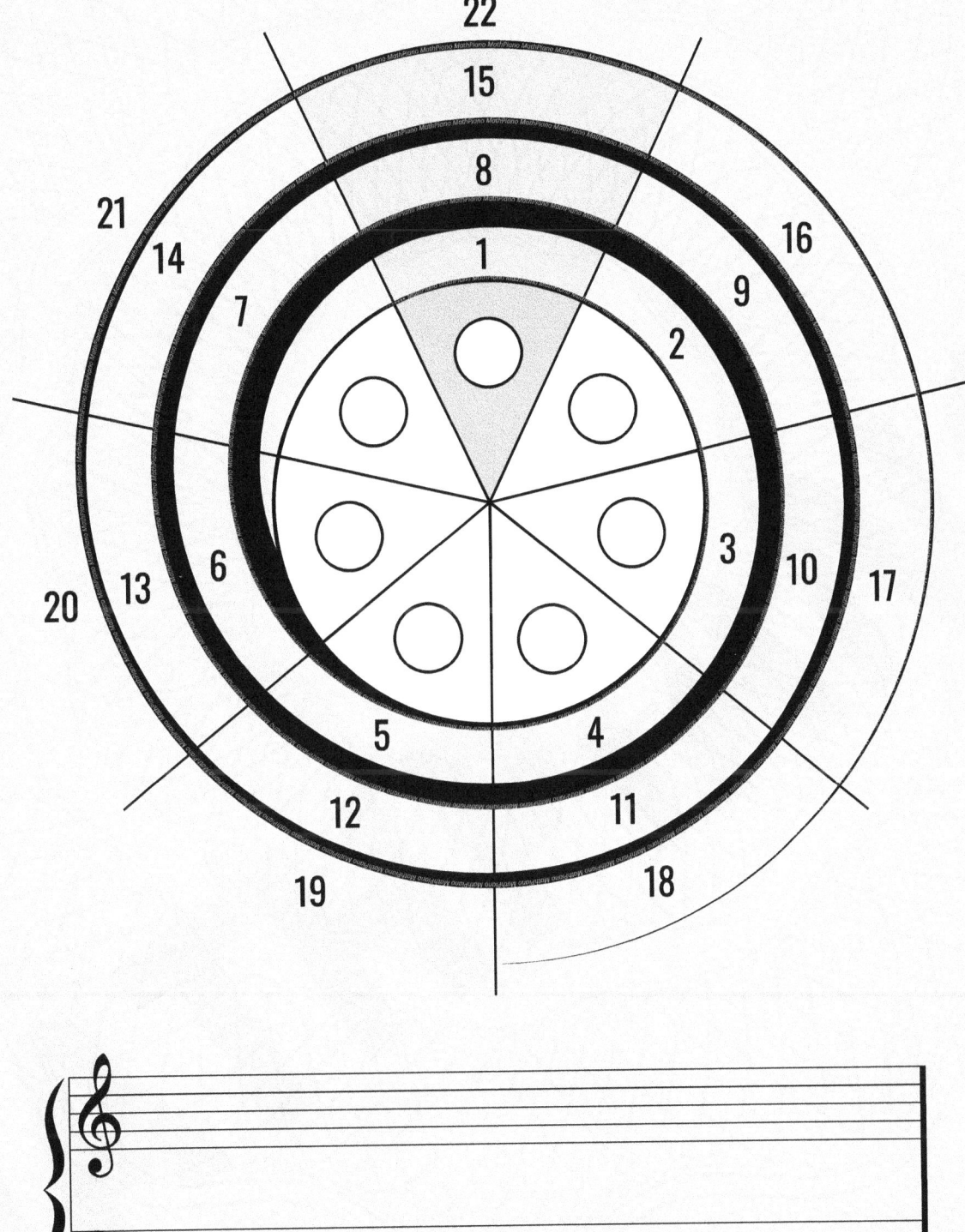

Key: C♯ Major

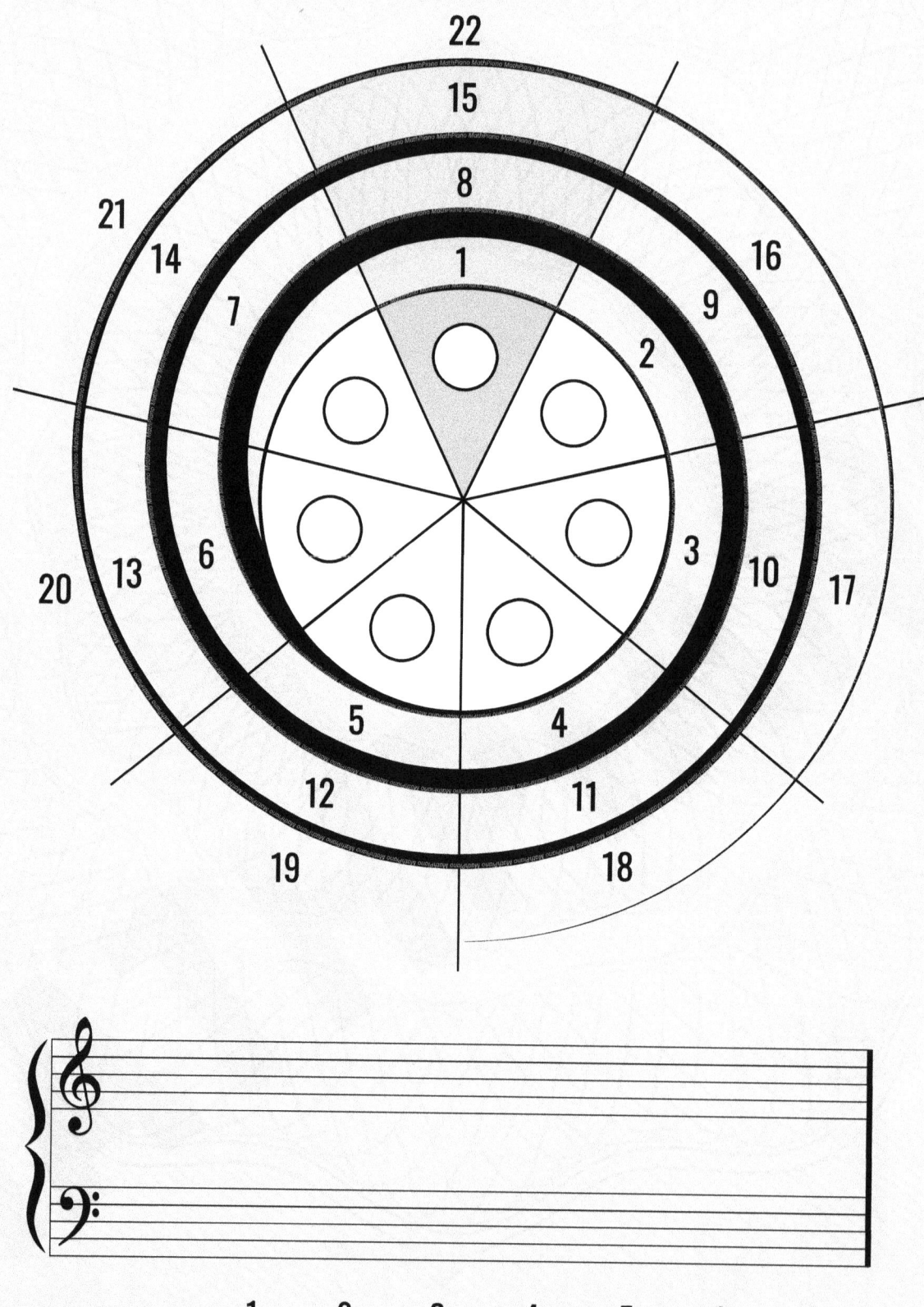

Key: A♯ Minor

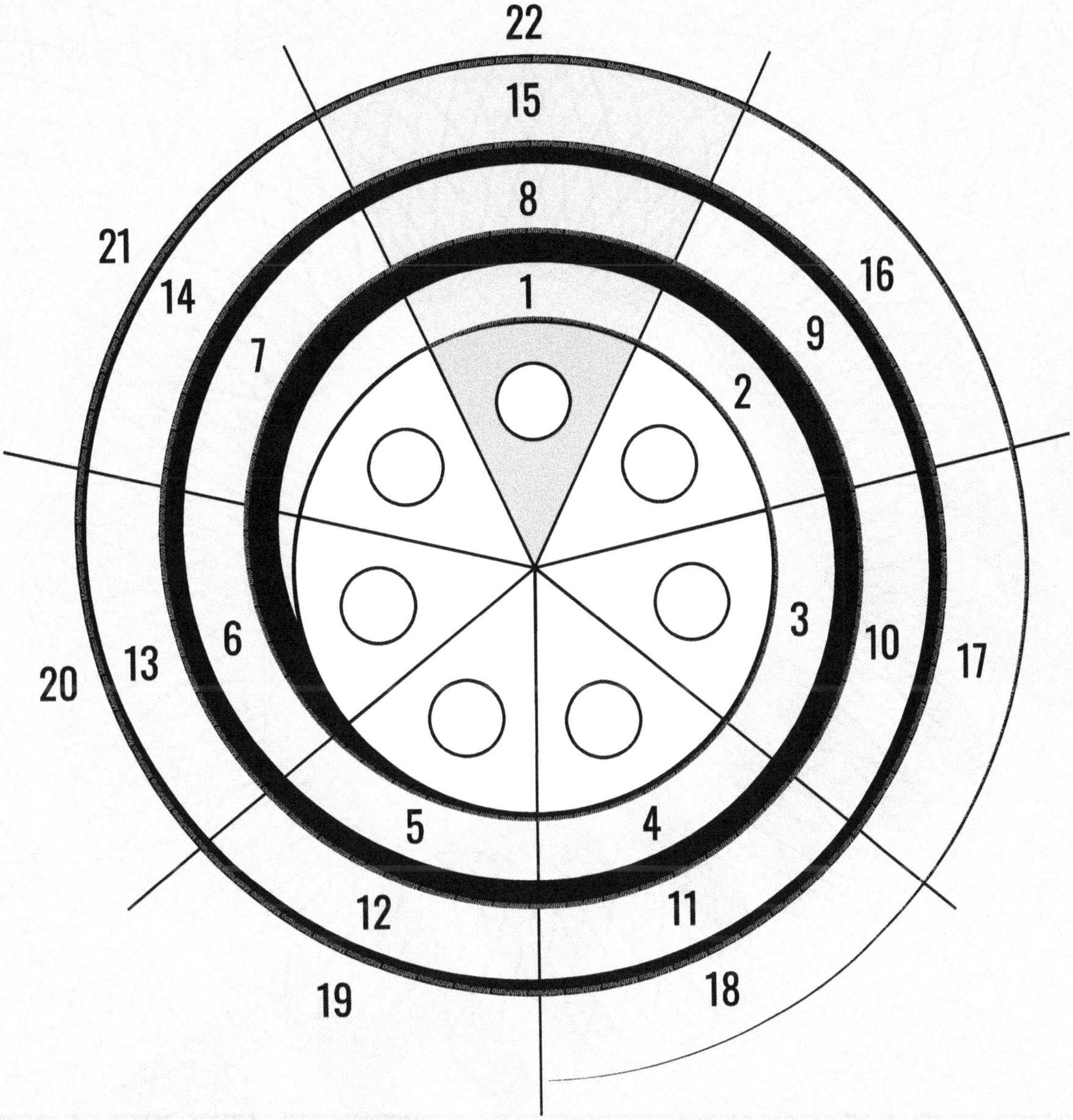

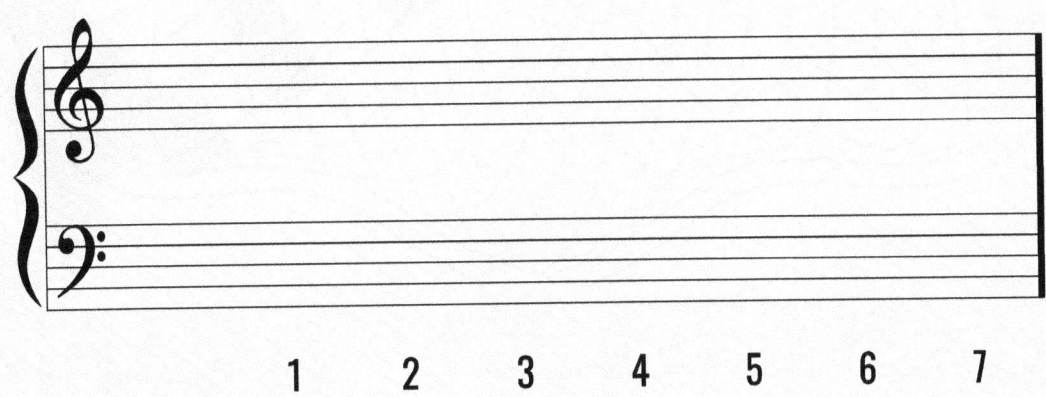

Key: F Major

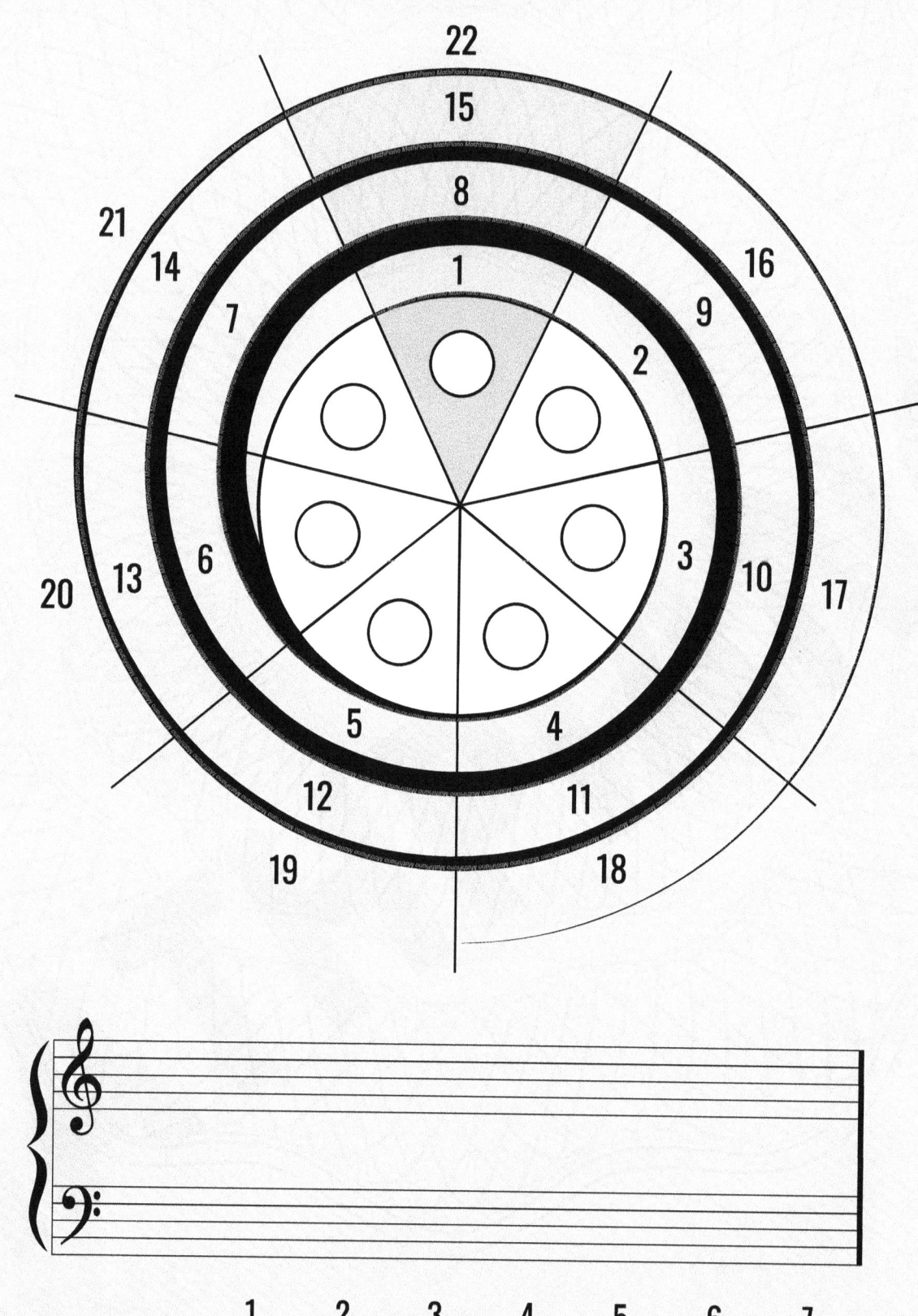

Key: D Minor

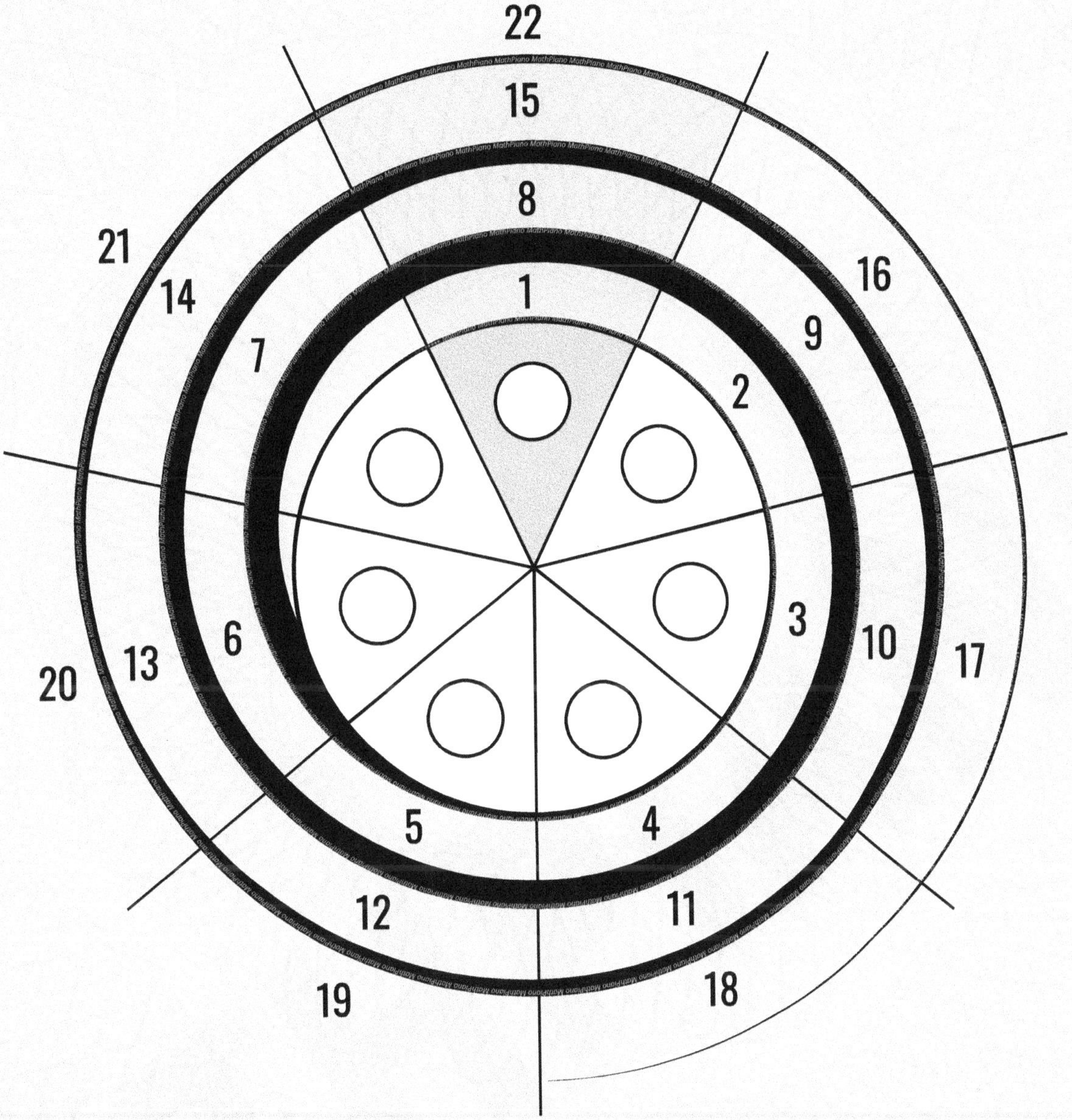

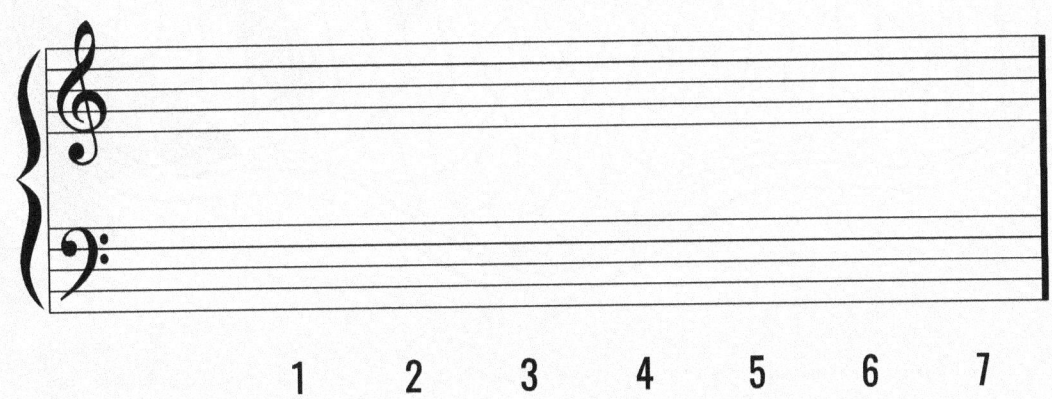

22
15
8
1
21
14
7
16
9
2
6
13
20
3
10
17
5
4
12
11
19
18

1 2 3 4 5 6 7

Key: B♭ Major

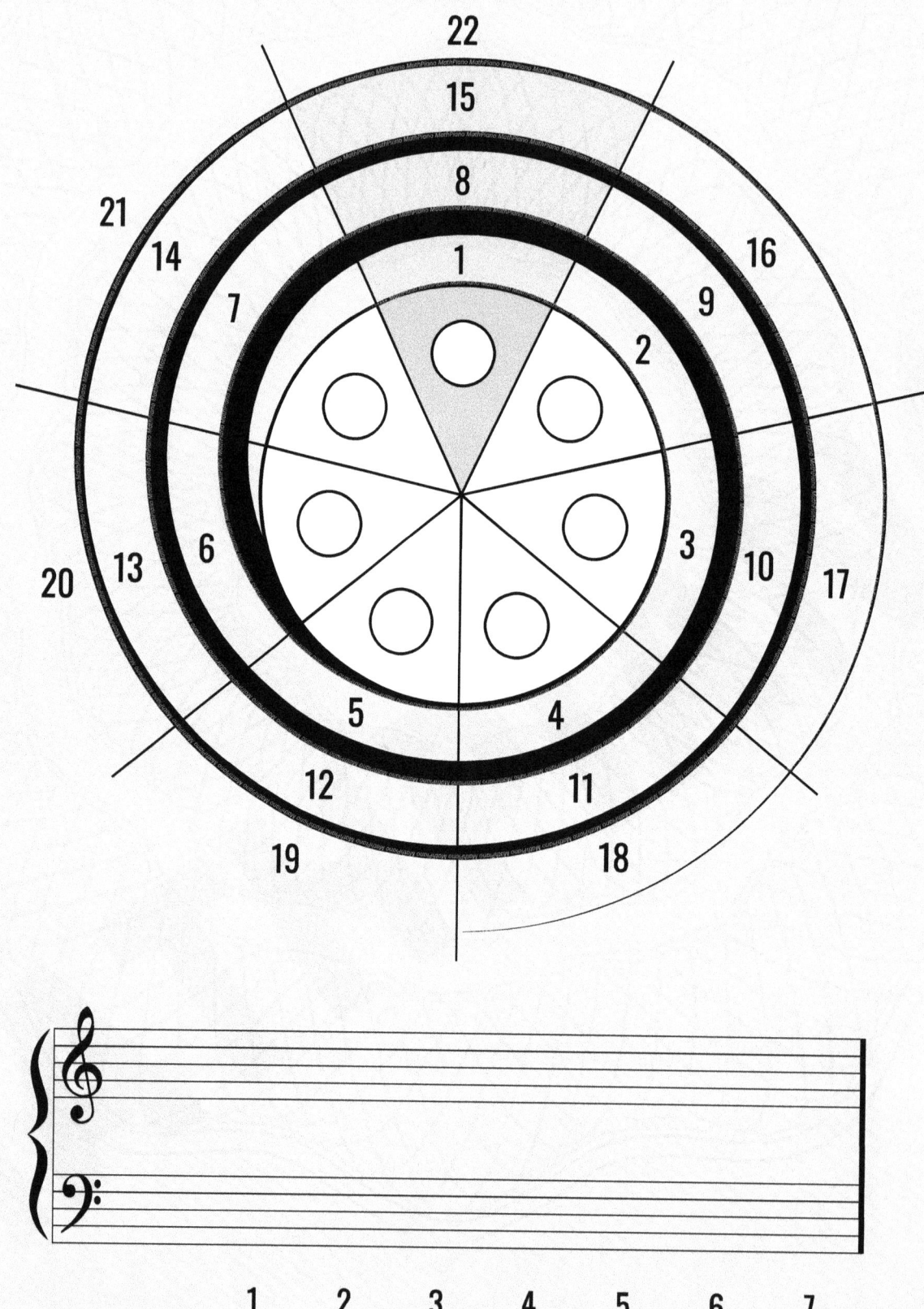

Key: G Minor

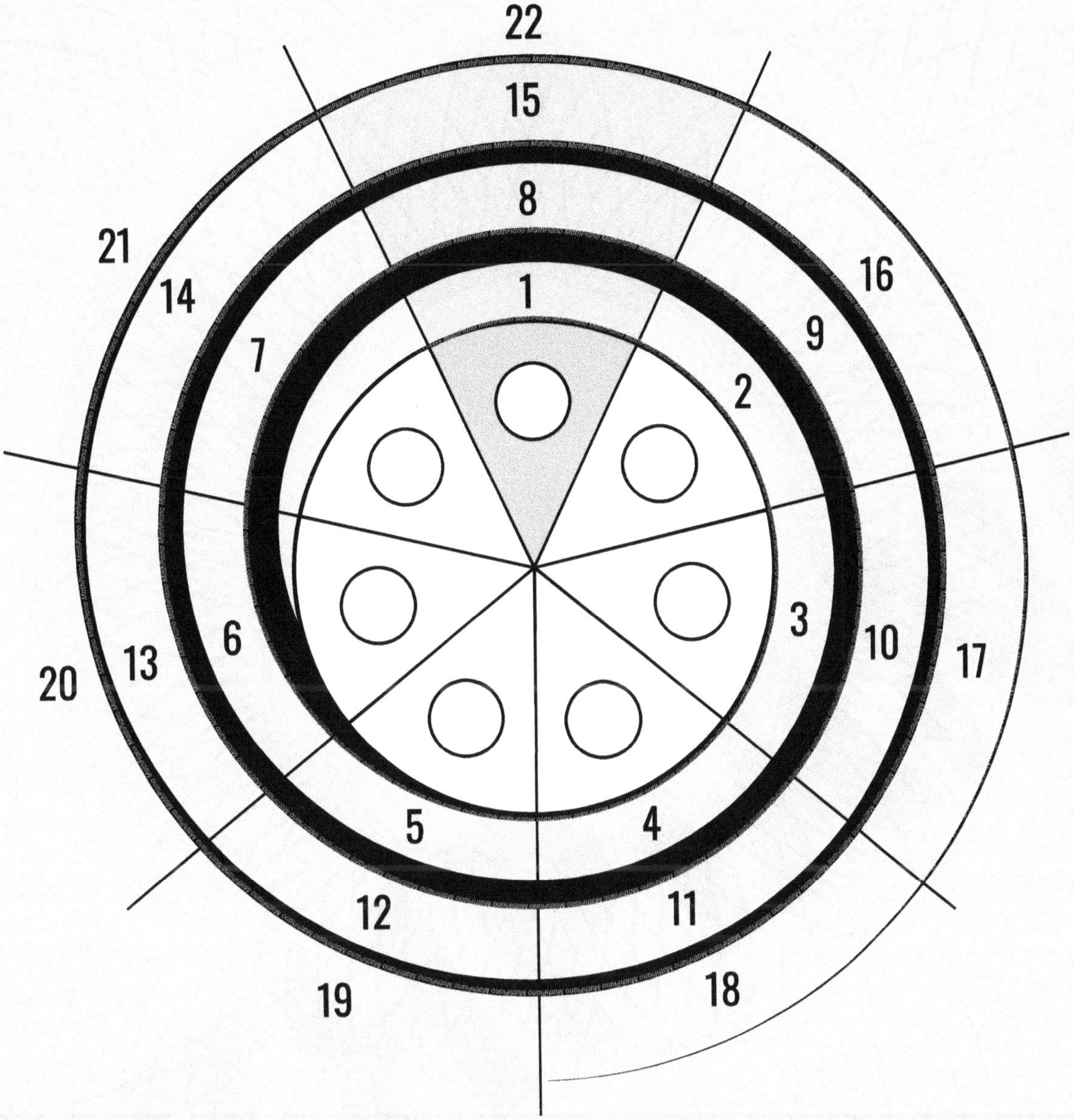

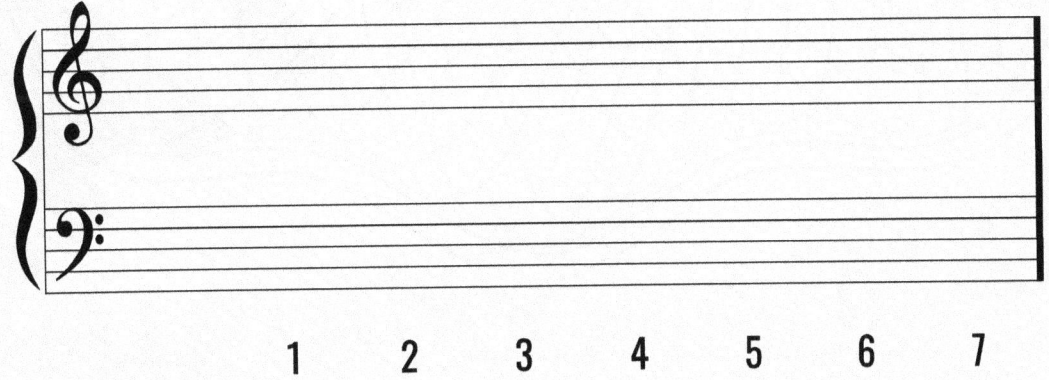

Key: E♭ Major

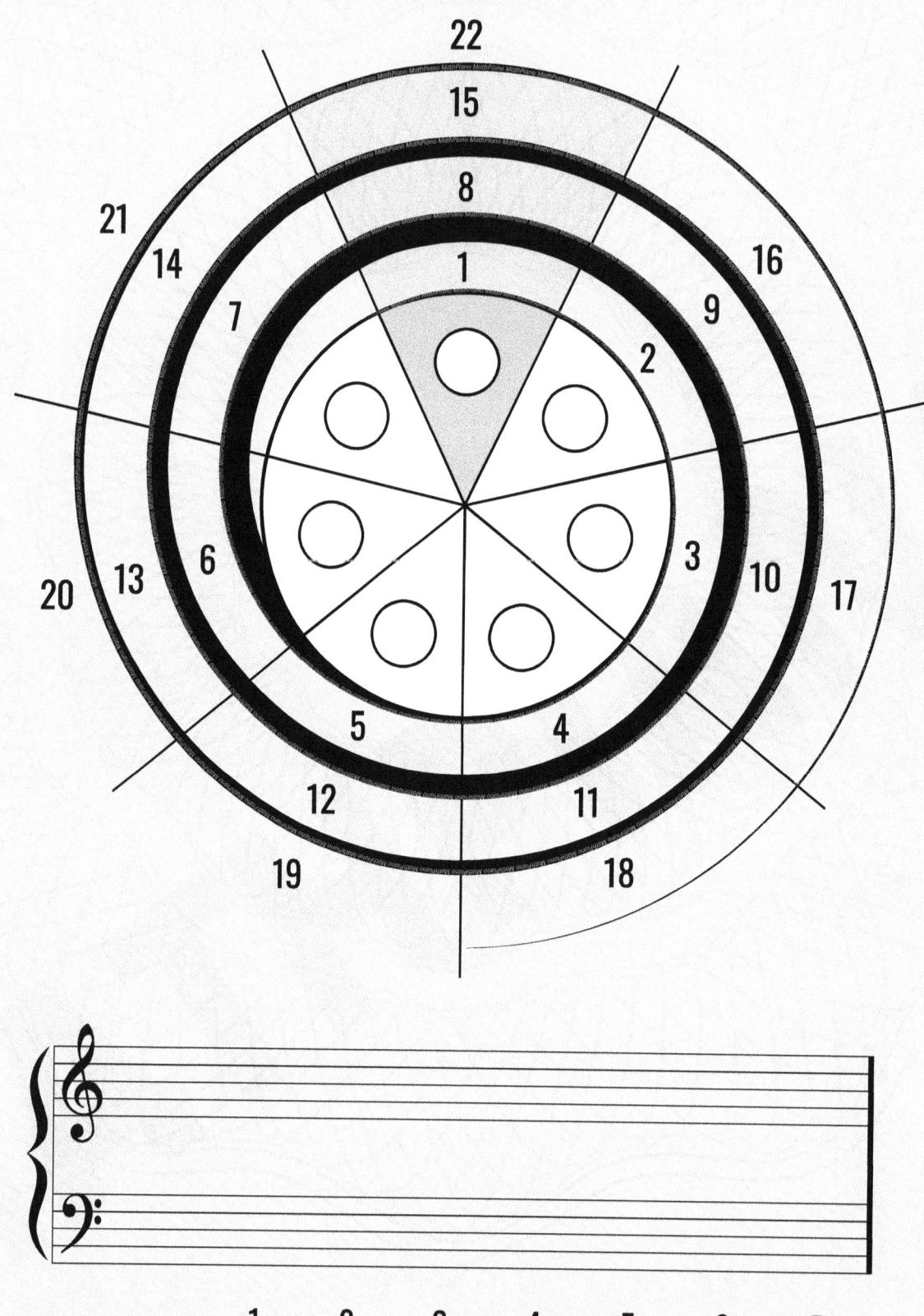

Key: C Minor

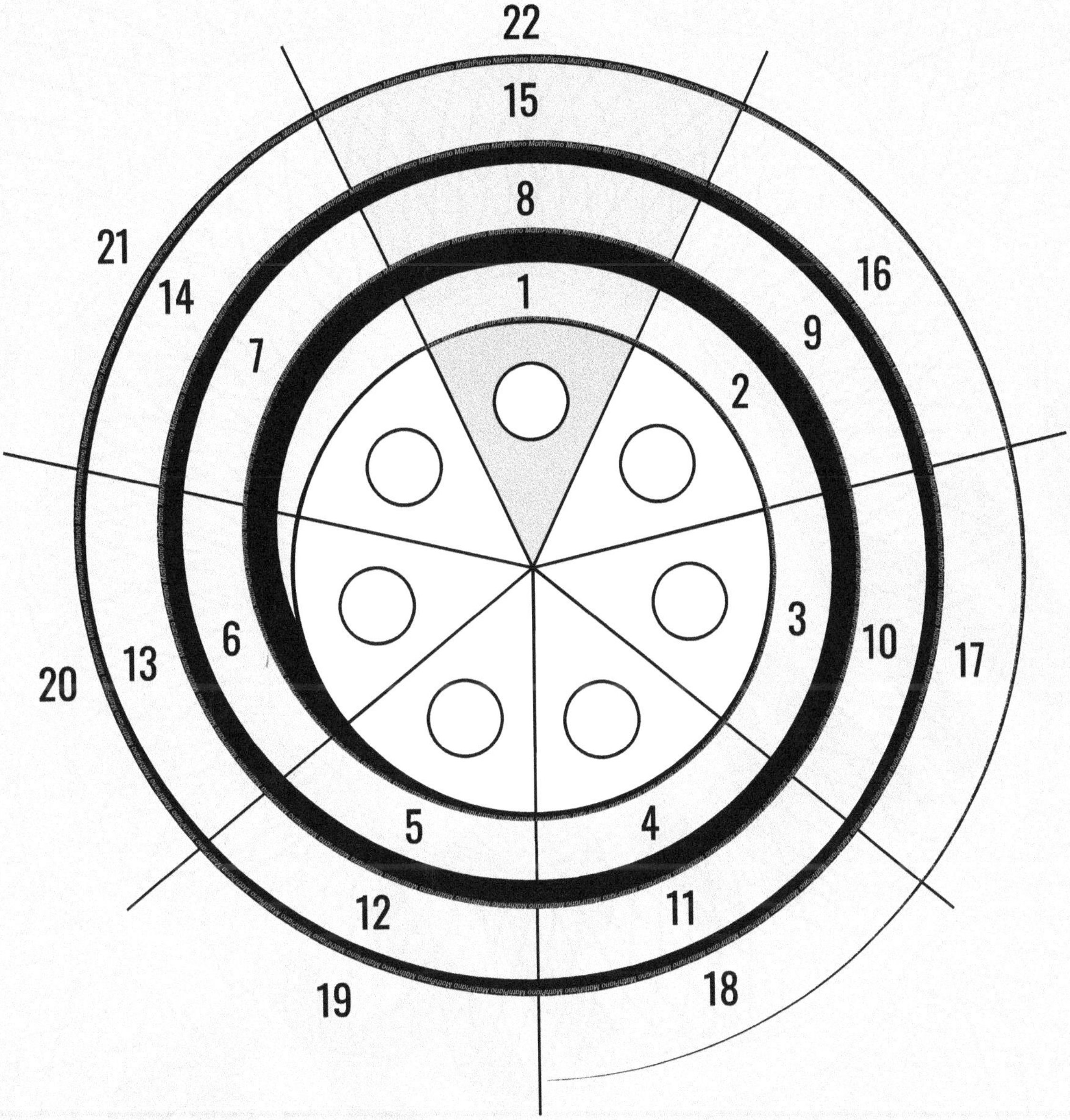

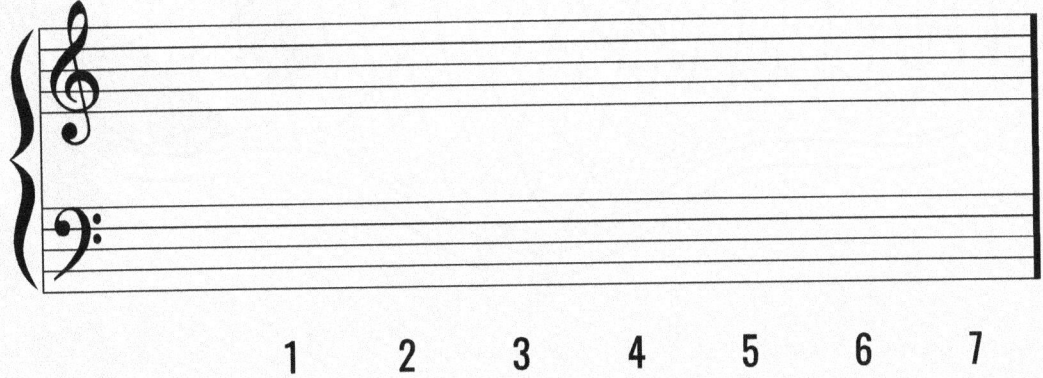

Key: A♭ Major

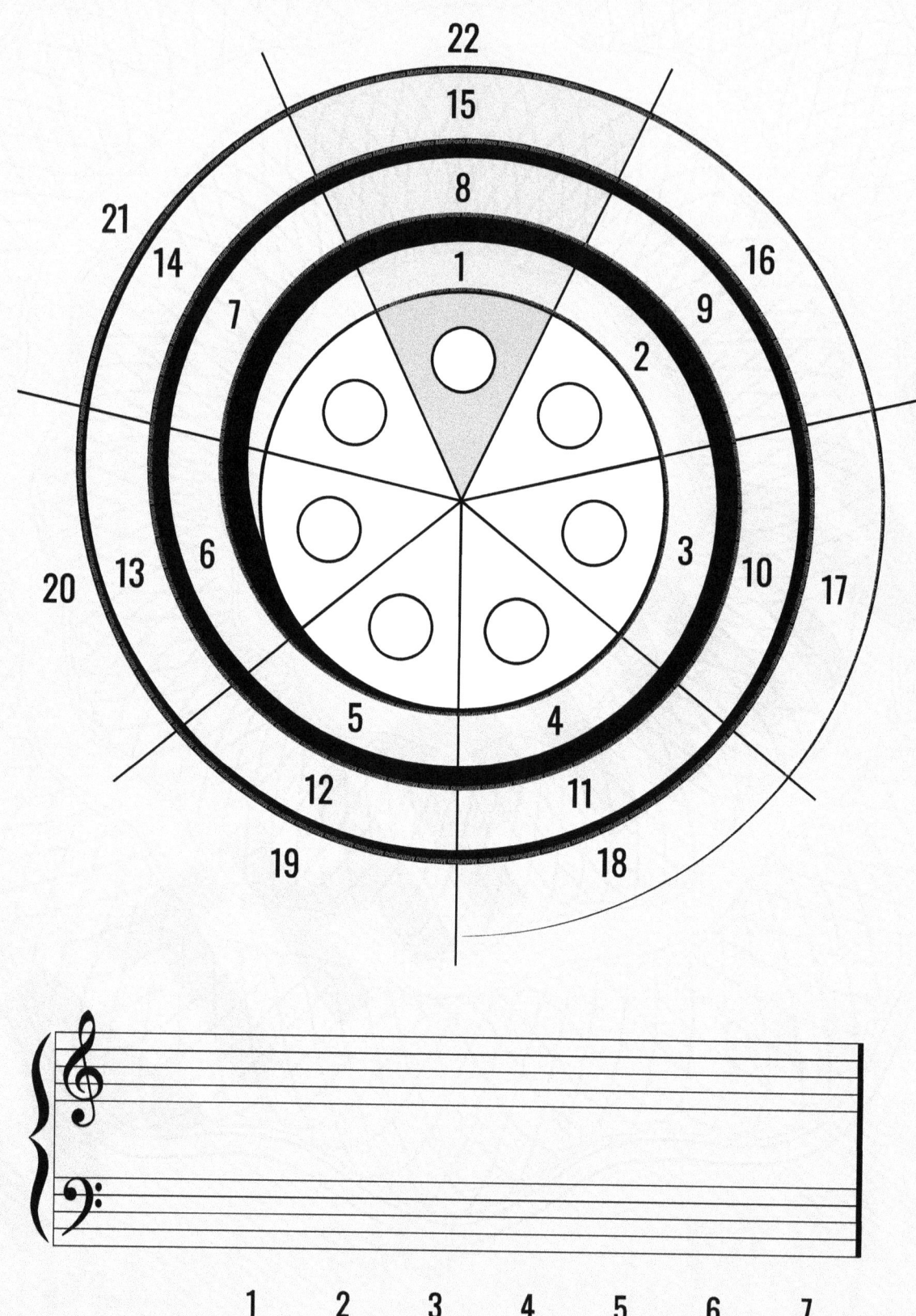

Key: F Minor

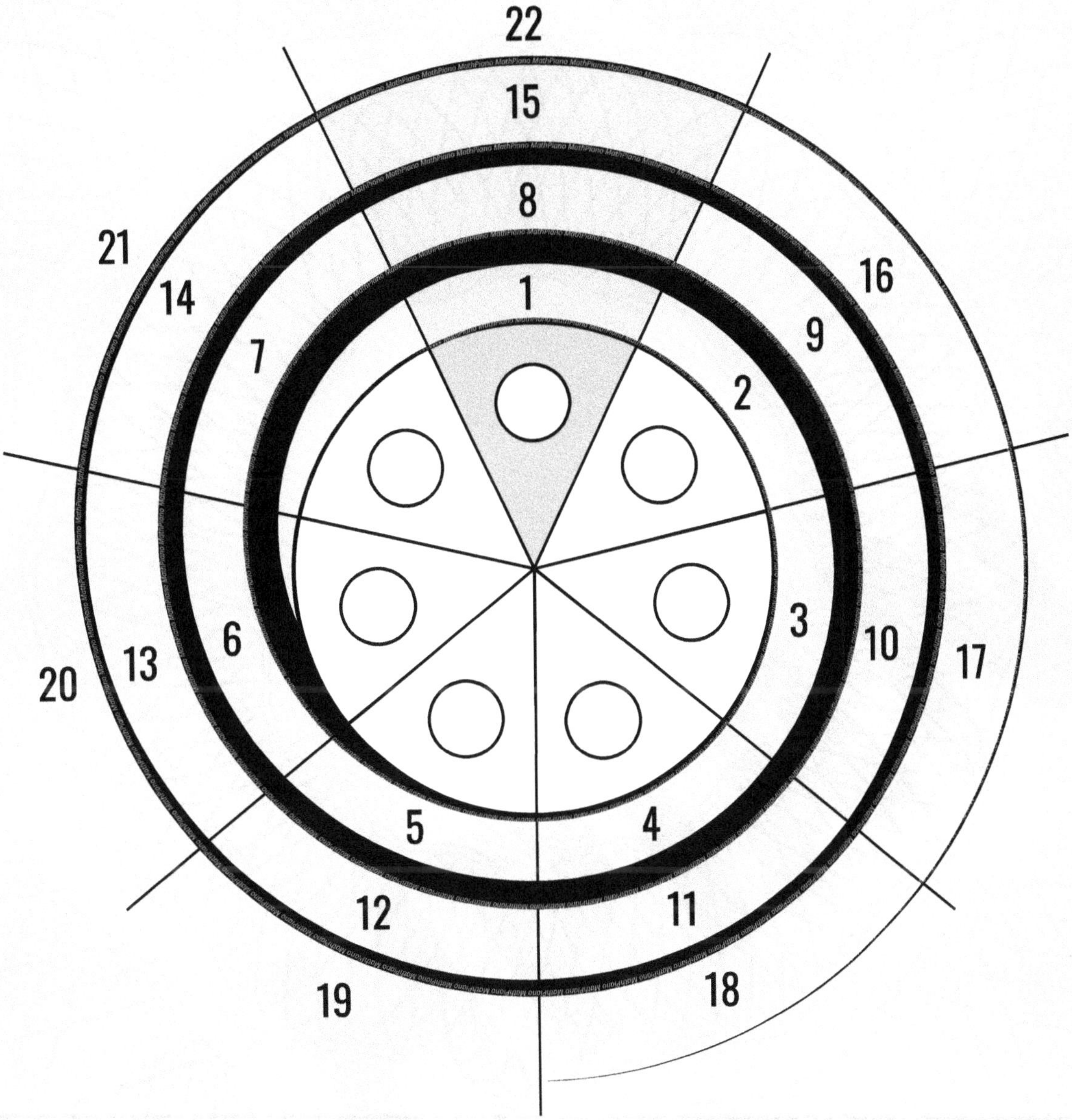

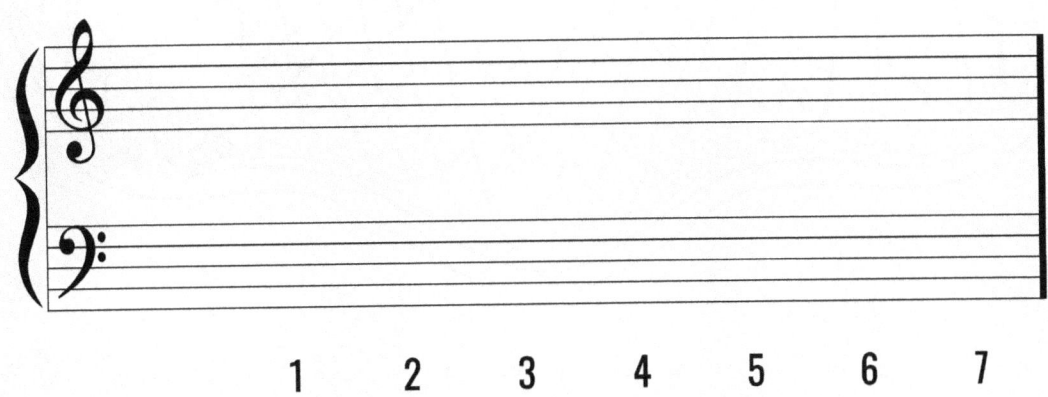

Key: D♭ Major

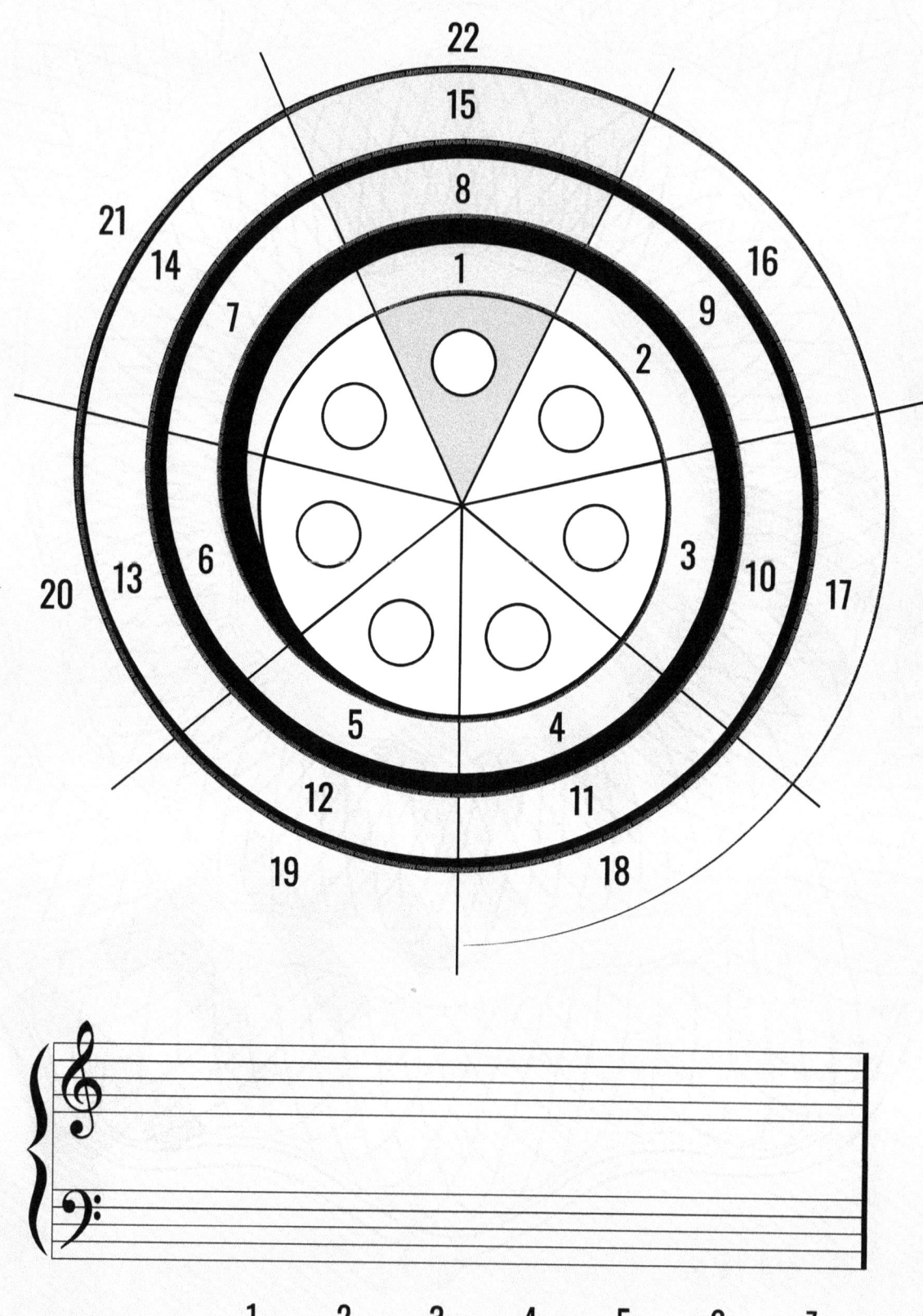

Key: B♭ Minor

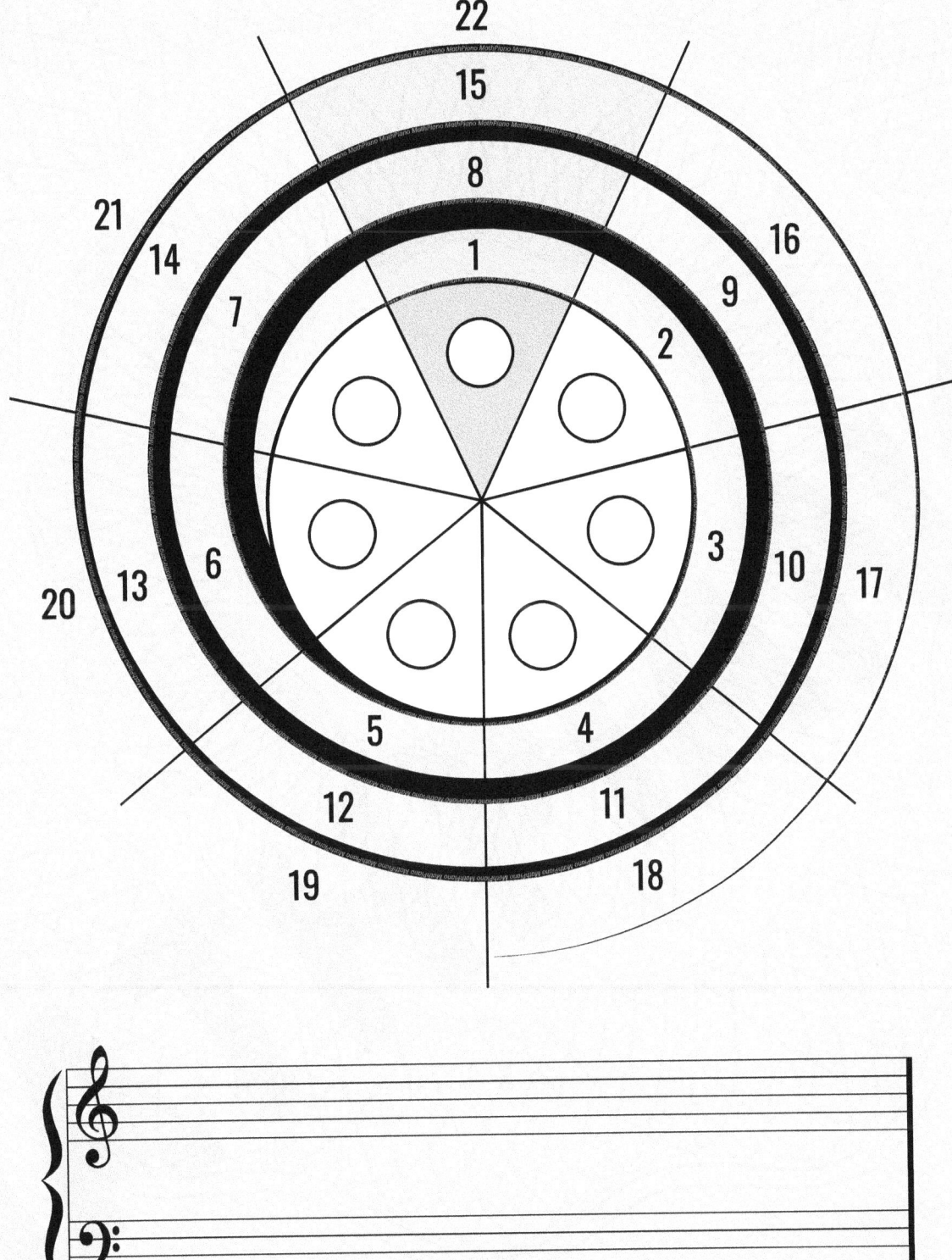

Key: G♭ Major

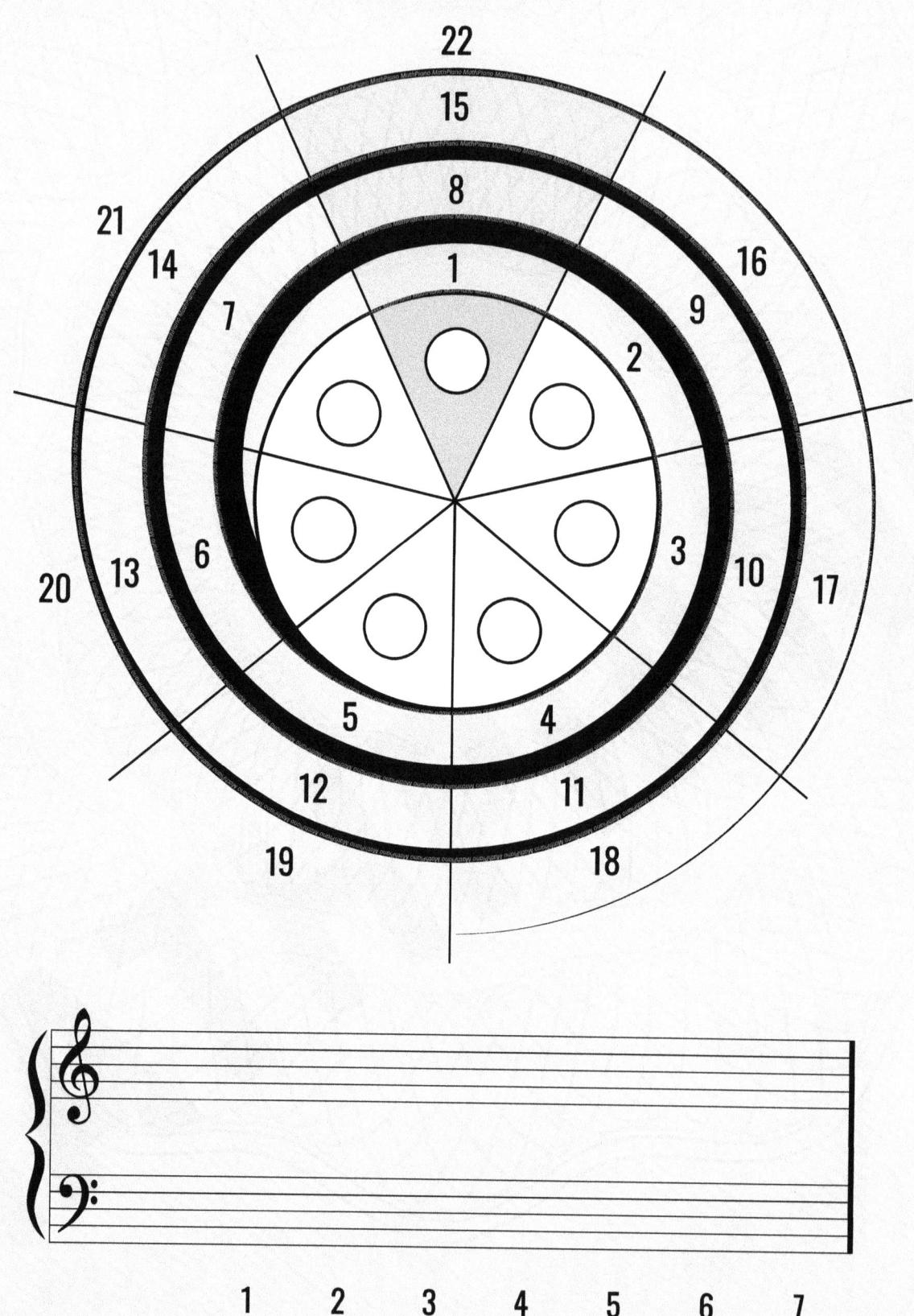

Key: E♭ Minor

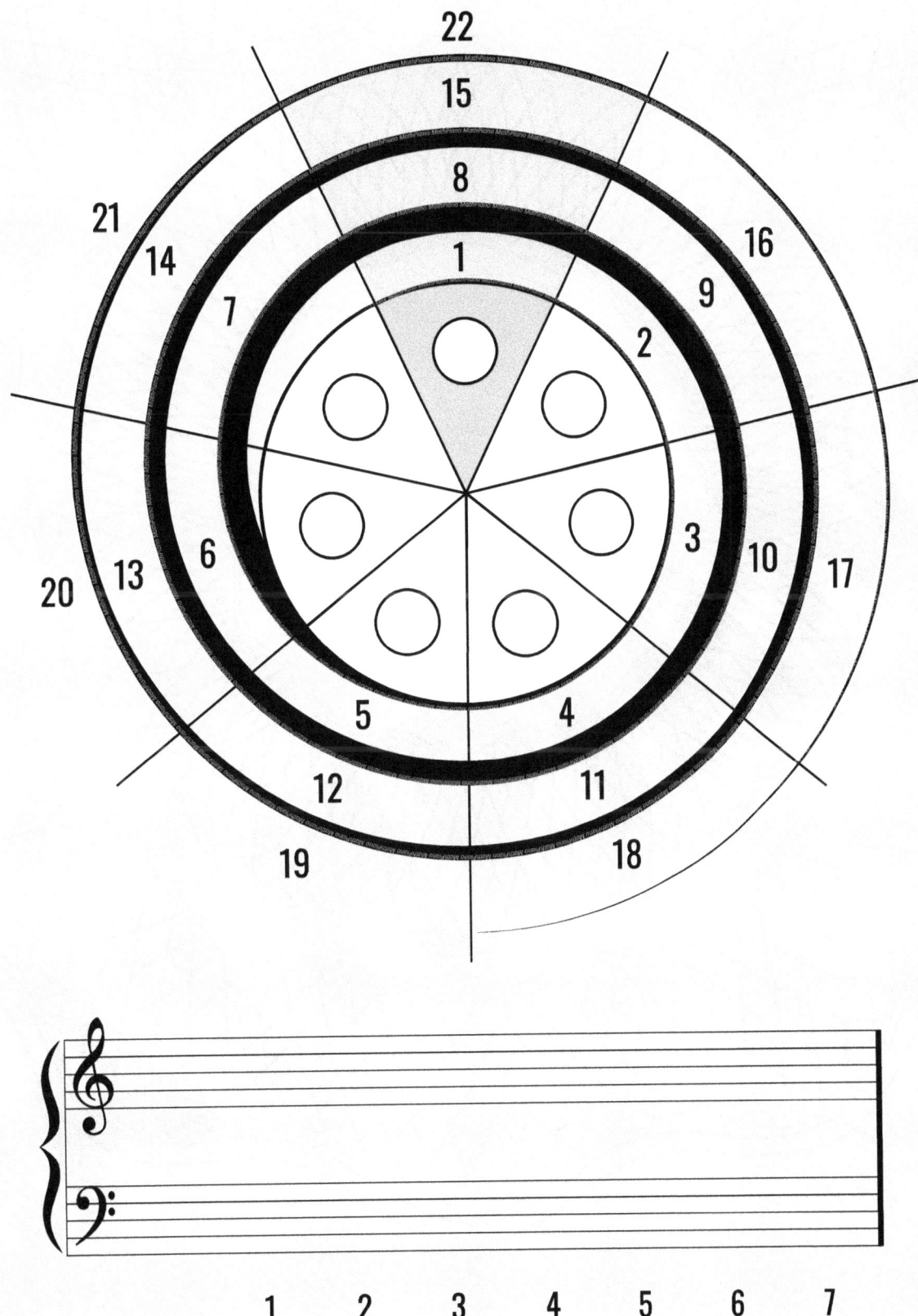

Key: C♭ Major

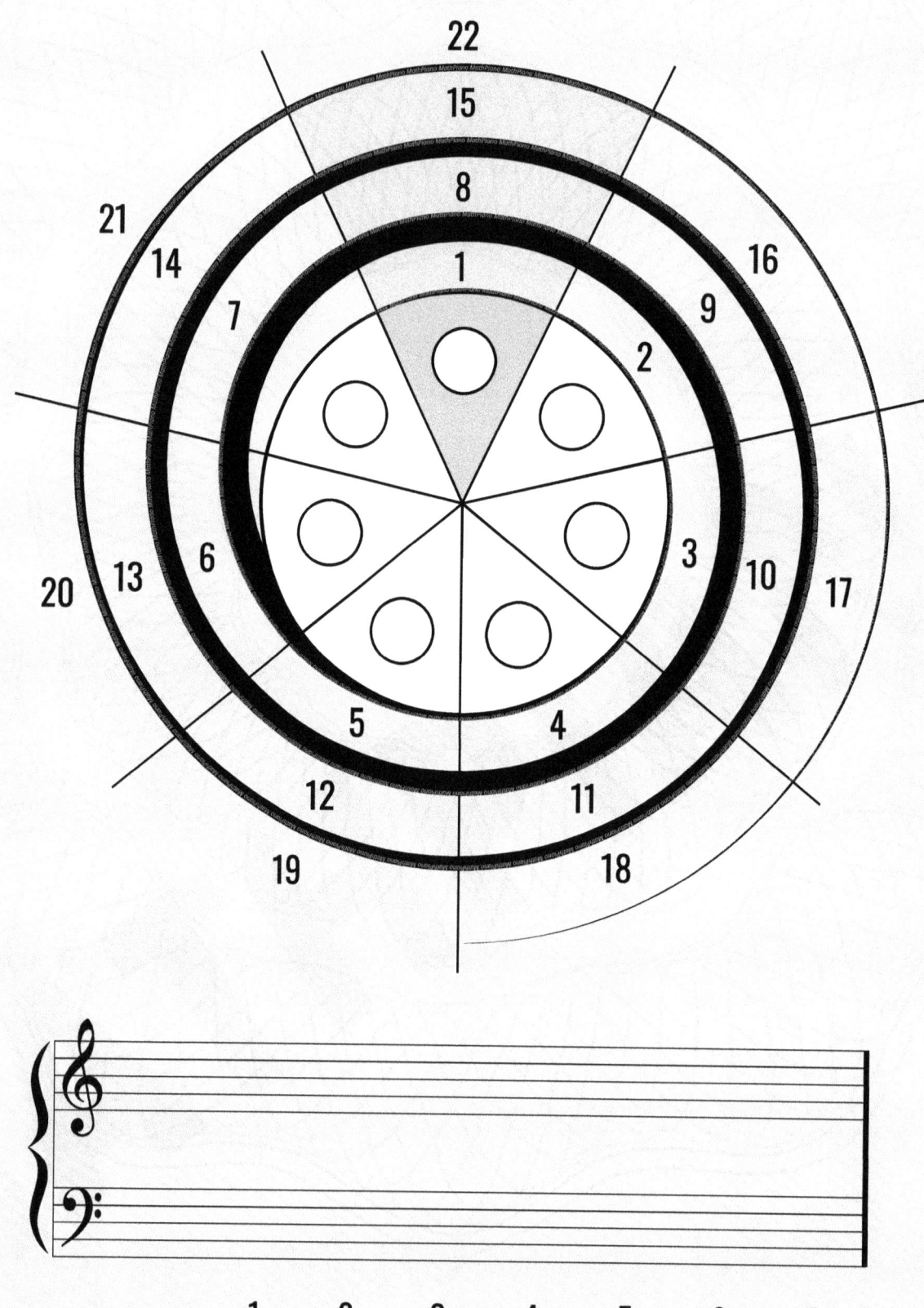

Key: A♭ Minor

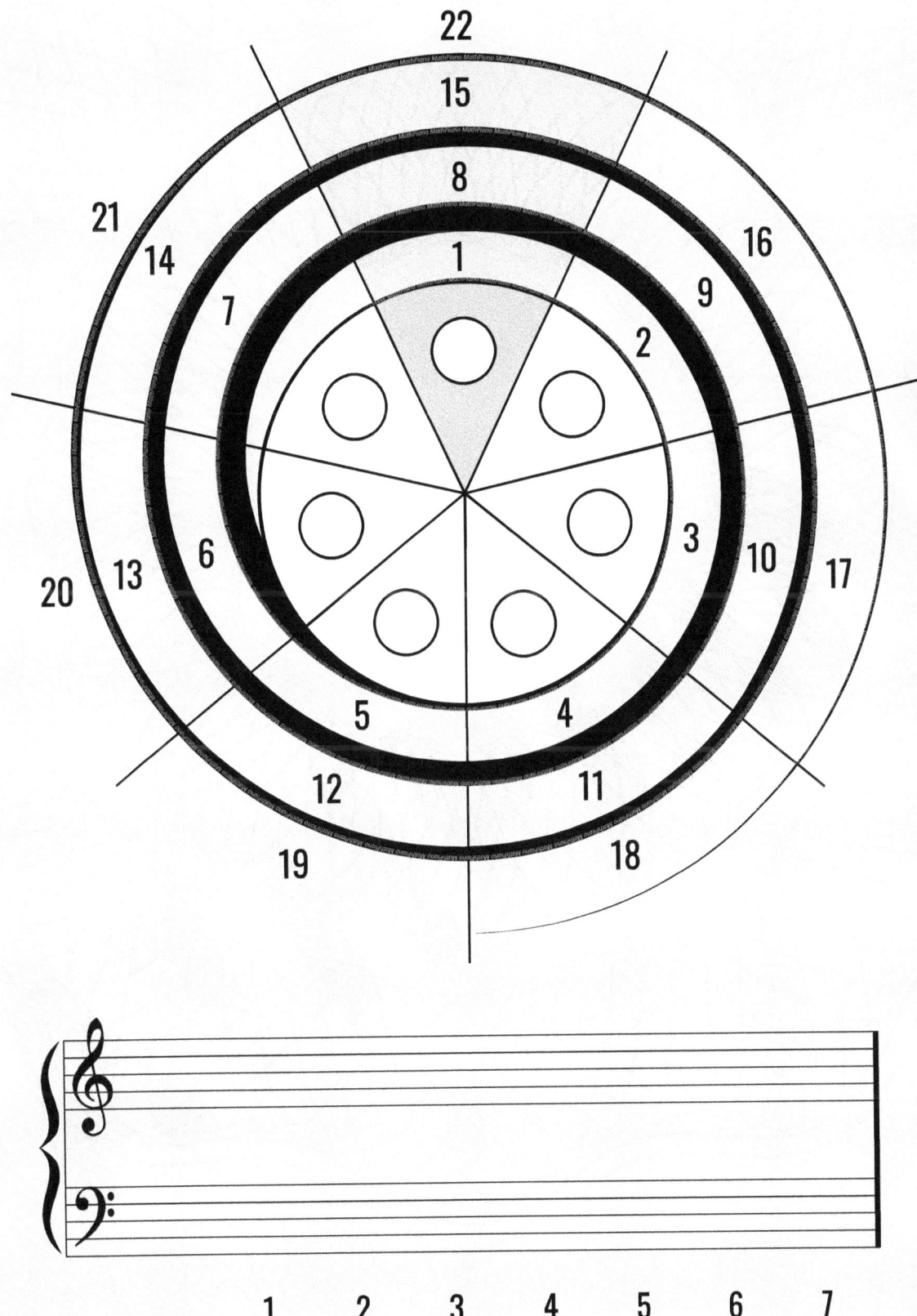

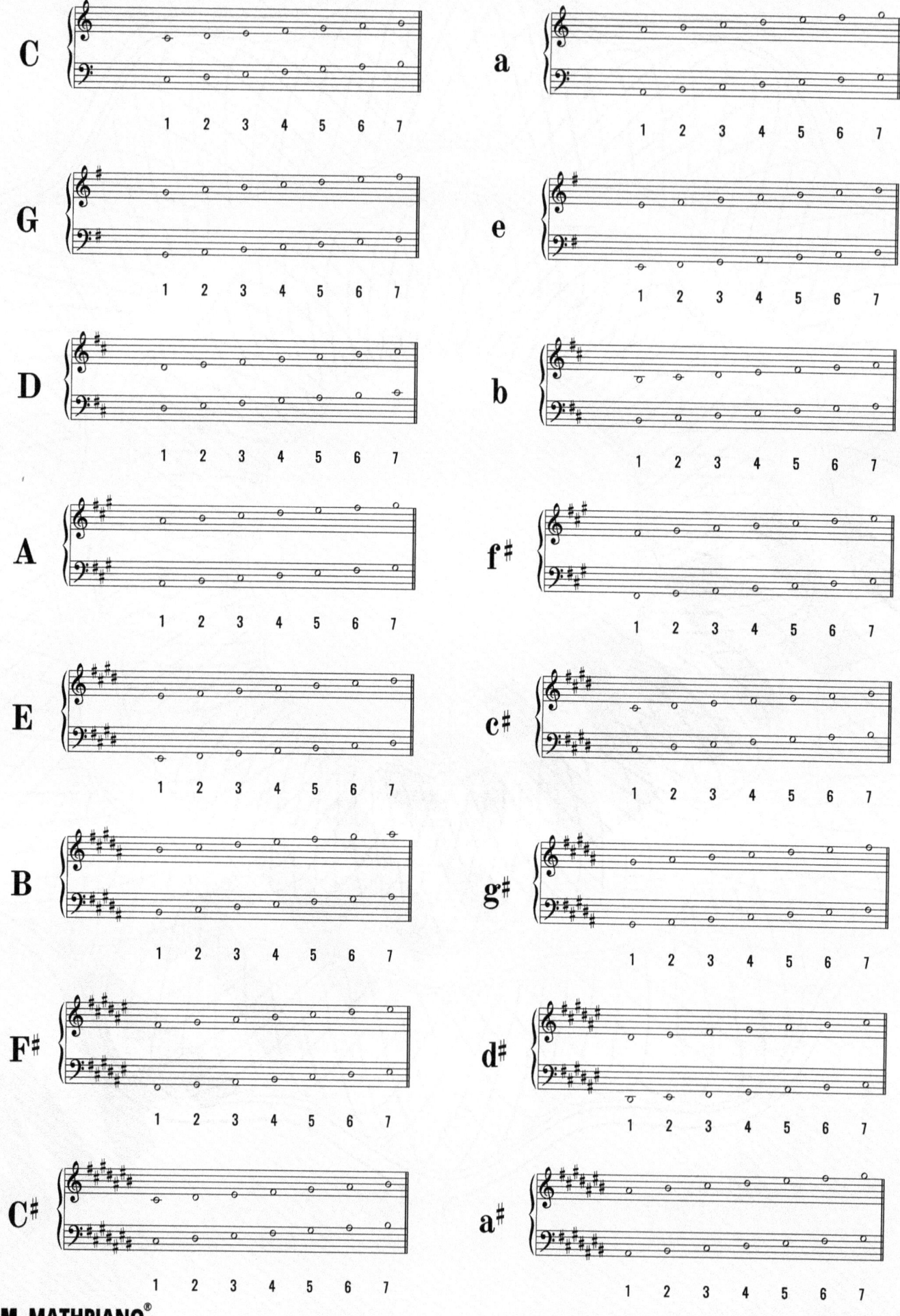

Reference

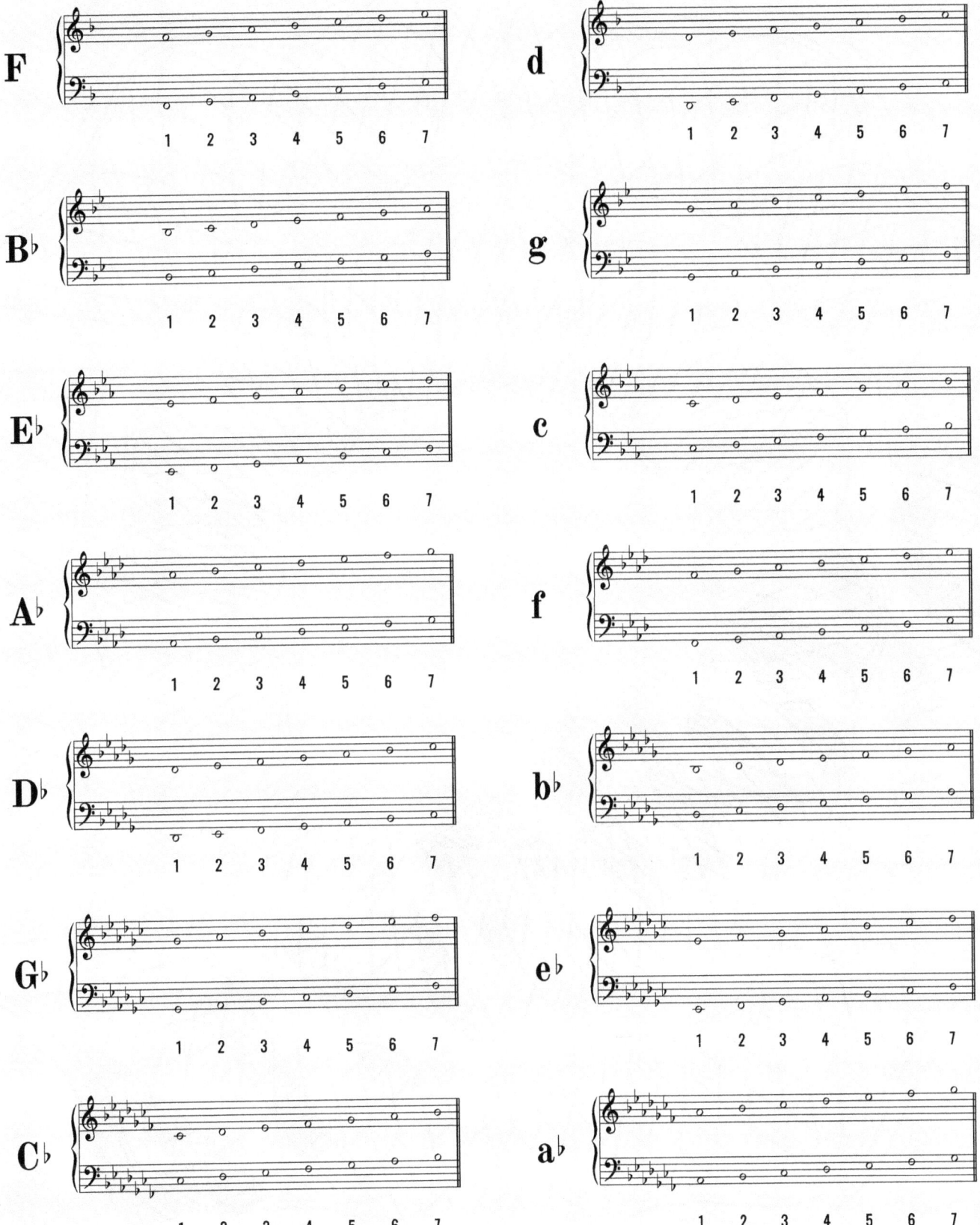

Reference

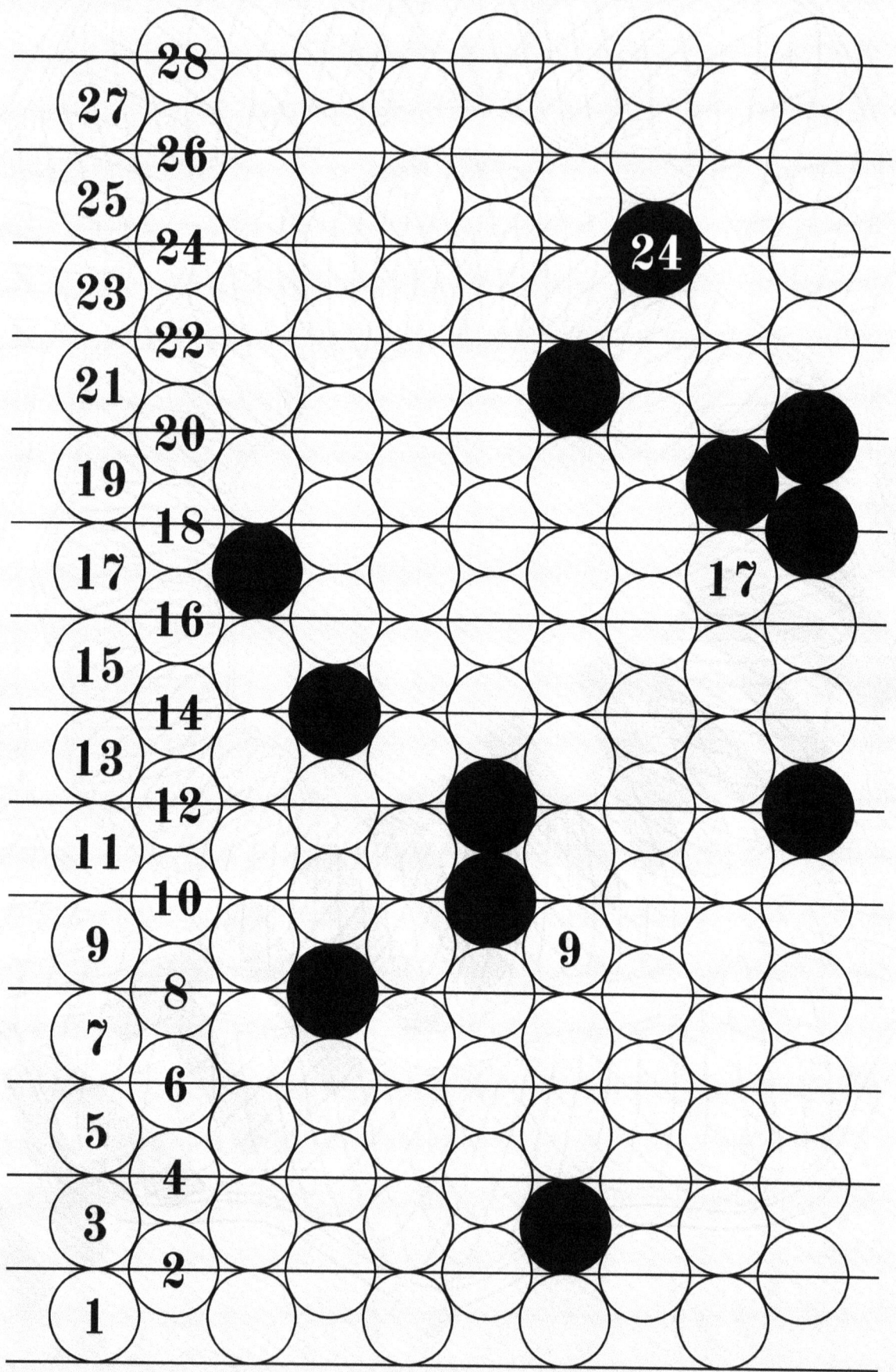